Declutter Your Life

Declutter Your Life

How Outer Order Leads to Inner Calm

Gill Hasson

CAPSTONE
A Wiley Brand

This edition first published 2018

© 2018 Gill Hasson

Registered office
John Wiley & Sons Ltd, The Atrium, Southern Gate, Chichester, West Sussex, PO19 8SQ, United Kingdom

For details of our global editorial offices, for customer services and for information about how to apply for permission to reuse the copyright material in this book please see our website at www.wiley.com.

The right of the author to be identified as the author of this work has been asserted in accordance with the Copyright, Designs and Patents Act 1988.

Wiley publishes in a variety of print and electronic formats and by print-on-demand. Some material included with standard print versions of this book may not be included in e-books or in print-on-demand. If this book refers to media such as a CD or DVD that is not included in the version you purchased, you may download this material at http://booksupport.wiley.com. For more information about Wiley products, visit www.wiley.com.

Designations used by companies to distinguish their products are often claimed as trademarks. All brand names and product names used in this book are trade names, service marks, trademarks or registered trademarks of their respective owners. The publisher is not associated with any product or vendor mentioned in this book.

Limit of Liability/Disclaimer of Warranty: While the publisher and author have used their best efforts in preparing this book, they make no representations or warranties with respect to the accuracy or completeness of the contents of this book and specifically disclaim any implied warranties of merchantability or fitness for a particular purpose. It is sold on the understanding that the publisher is not engaged in rendering professional services and neither the publisher nor the author shall be liable for damages arising herefrom. If professional advice or other expert assistance is required, the services of a competent professional should be sought.

Library of Congress Cataloging-in-Publication Data

Names: Hasson, Gill, author.
Title: Declutter your life : how outer order leads to inner calm / Gill
   Hasson.
Description: Chichester, West Sussex, United Kingdom : Wiley, 2018. |
   Includes bibliographical references and index. |
Identifiers: LCCN 2017044532 (print) | ISBN 9780857087379 (pbk.)
Subjects: LCSH: Storage in the home. | Orderliness. | Time management. |
   House cleaning.
Classification: LCC TX309 .H37 2018 (print) | DDC 648/.8–dc23
LC record available at https://lccn.loc.gov/2017044532
A catalogue record for this book is available from the British Library.

ISBN 978-0-857-08737-9 (pbk) ISBN 978-0-857-08738-6 (ebk)
ISBN 978-0-857-08736-2 (ebk)

Cover design/image: Wiley

Set in 11/14 pt SabonLTStd-Roman by Aptara Inc., New Delhi, India

Printed in Great Britain by CPI Group (UK) Ltd, Croydon CR0 4YY

10 9 8 7 6 5 4 3 2 1

Contents

Introduction

A couple of years ago, we were watching TV when we heard a loud bang. We rushed upstairs expecting to see that a piece of furniture had collapsed and fallen over, but neither my husband nor I could find anything that explained the loud noise.

A few days later, though, I noticed the ceiling was dipping in one corner of our bedroom. We called a builder. When he climbed down from the loft of our three-bedroom semi-detached Victorian house, he told us that a rafter had snapped – that we were lucky the ceiling hadn't fallen in on top of us while we slept. 'You've got so much stuff up there', he said. 'Victorian lofts weren't designed to store stuff.' Of course they weren't. The Victorians didn't have anything to store. We did.

Our sons had grown up and two of them had left home. Amongst other things, one son had put a bike up in the loft (which, when I phoned to ask him about it, he told me he didn't want any more. That I could get rid of it. Not him. Me.) I'd kept two large boxes of Lego, a box of trains and train track, a box of Brio, two large boxes of other toys and children's books, the wooden castle my Dad made for the boys and an inflatable dinghy we bought for a holiday in Devon, which they used once – 10 years ago. Then there was my husband's large vinyl collection, a stereo, twelve boxes of negatives from his career as a freelance photographer, my photo albums, my wedding dress, my university essays, a box of letters, odd bits of furniture, two rugs, lighting, extra glasses and large dishes for parties. We had lots of camping gear and Christmas decorations. And those are just the things I can remember that we brought out of the loft when we had to completely empty it so that the rafter could be fixed and the loft insulated.

We're not hoarders. We're just a normal family. We'd lived in the same house for 20 years and brought up three sons. We had all the same type of stuff as any family who have studied, had jobs, been on holidays, camped, gone to festivals, celebrated Christmas, had parties, enjoyed music and books and had a variety of interests.

Once we'd emptied the loft I realized the rest of the house had plenty more things that we'd held onto for whatever reason: in case we needed it, because we hoped we'd need it, because it would feel wrong to chuck it out or because we just couldn't be bothered to clear it out.

Do you also have too much stuff?

Clutter can silently creep up on you and, before you know it, you've accumulated a lot of junk and jumble and all sorts of objects and oddments. It becomes overwhelming, but for one reason or another you hang onto it.

What can you do and where do you start? The key to managing clutter is to get to the root of the problem: your own thinking. *Declutter Your Life* explains how to change your relationship with the things you own and think about your things in a new light; in a way that is constructive, will help you to identify what is and isn't clutter and enable you to let the clutter go.

Most of our things started out as something useful, interesting, attractive. But in time – over the months and years – the things we've bought or acquired reach a point where they're no longer useful or enjoyable. They're clutter. Instead of hanging on to and being weighed down with objects and possessions that keep you stuck in the past, you can learn to think about your things in a way that's constructive and helpful to you.

There are plenty of tips and techniques and lots of advice in this book to help you. You'll discover how outer order leads to inner calm; you'll feel less overwhelmed and stressed, there'll be less to think about, organize and clean. Instead – as I did – you'll feel more in control and have more time and energy for what's actually important to you in terms of other people, your work and other interests in your life.

Part 2 of this book goes on to explain how the principles and steps taken to declutter and simplify your living space can improve not just your home but also other aspects of your life: your commitments, your friends, your work and the information you take in.

You'll discover that, like your possessions, your commitments and friends can also keep you stuck in the past. You'll learn that if you want to let go of commitments and friendships that no longer fit with your life, you *can* do so without feeling guilty. Who and what was right for you then is not necessarily right now. Don't let the past dictate the present! What matters is what commitments and friends you choose to keep now.

Whether it's too many commitments, friends you no longer have anything in common with, work that leaves you no time to breathe or a bombardment of information, it's time to declutter; to let go, simplify and make room for the new.

PART 1

Declutter Your Home

Have nothing in your house that you do not know to be useful, or believe to be beautiful.

William Morris

1
How Do You Accumulate So Much?

The world is too much with us; late and soon,
Getting and spending, we lay waste our powers; –
Little we see in Nature that is ours;
We have given our hearts away, a sordid boon!

William Wordsworth

'The world is too much with us.' It certainly is. So many of us have more things than we could ever need: clothes we've never worn or haven't worn in ages; CDs, cassette tapes, records, games, consoles, phones and miscellaneous cords to tech devices; books we've read and won't read again; magazines with articles we're going to read but actually never get round to; trinkets, ornaments and family heirlooms left behind by past generations; gifts you've never liked, board games you no longer play; things that need cleaning or repair before you can use them again; pots, pans, utensils, kit and equipment you just don't use.

You're not a hoarder – you're just a normal person with lots of stuff.

Maybe you've a stockpile of cleaning and food supplies: cans, jars and packets of food? A freezer jammed full with most of the food staying there week after week, month after month? And in the bathroom – a test lab worth of potions and lotions? Stuff just seems to be piling up: old letters and bills, children's toys, arts and crafts – all on tables and worktops and shoved inside cupboards, wardrobes, sheds and shelves.

Do you think your home is too small or you need more storage space? It's unlikely. What's more likely is that you just have too much stuff. A bigger home and more storage space – cupboards, wardrobes, chests, storage boxes etc – would just give you more reasons to accumulate and keep stuff.

Get stuff. Buy stuff. Keep it. Get more of it. Keep that, too. When did this become normal?

In the past, it appears that most people lived their lives with scarcity. Material goods – clothes, furniture, books, toys etc. – were not only hard to come by, they were expensive. If you could acquire something, you got it and kept hold of it.

But now, in Western countries especially, we live in abundance: things are relatively inexpensive and easy to acquire. Not only do we have a plentiful supply of the things we need and want, we have an unlimited supply and we're keeping it all; filling our homes and lives. We seem to have dramatically increased the amount of things we own, without really noticing that it was happening.

Having too much stuff is the new normal.

'Contemporary U.S. households have more possessions per household than any society in global history', explains Jeanne E. Arnold, Professor of anthropology at the University of California, Los Angeles. In 2012, Professor Arnold and a team of sociologists and anthropologists published their book, *Life at Home in the Twenty-First Century*, based on a four-year study of 32 middle-class, dual-income families in Los Angeles.

Three-quarters of the families had stopped using their garages to park their cars. They had too much stuff crammed in 'to make way for rejected furniture and cascading bins and boxes of mostly forgotten household goods'. The families had enough food to survive all manner of disasters; 47% had second fridges. A few of the families had more TVs than people.

The families gained 30% more possessions with the arrival of each child. But instead of bringing satisfaction and contentment and making the world better, those who regarded their homes as 'cluttered' reported feeling stressed by it all. These people weren't on a TV show about hoarding. They were just 'average' families.

Yes, all the families were in the US. But is it really that much different in the UK or any other Western country? Back in 2010, British toy manufacturer Dream Town commissioned research to discover what toys children own and regularly play with.

The study found that the average 10-year-old owns 238 toys but parents estimated that their children play with just 12 'favourites' – 5% – on a daily basis. The study of 3000 parents also revealed that more than half thought their children ended up playing with the same toys day in and day out because they had too many to choose from.

They have too much stuff! *We* have too much stuff! Stuff that takes up space, thought, energy and time or money without providing any real benefit.

A house is just a pile of stuff with a cover on it.

George Carlin

Sometimes, it feels like the items on our shelves, in our cupboards, in sheds, lofts and garages manage to reproduce and multiply when our backs are turned.

Is your kitchen so cluttered there's no room to cook? Is the lack of storage in your bathroom driving you crazy? Is your wardrobe bursting at the seams? You think that it's because your home is too small or you don't have enough storage space. Maybe you've never once blamed having too much stuff as being the problem.

How do we accumulate so much stuff?

So how do we manage to accumulate so much stuff? Through shopping trips, markets and car boot sales; with online shopping on Amazon, Gumtree and eBay etc. Then there are Christmas and birthday gifts, things we inherit and souvenirs we pick up from our holidays.

Most of our clutter doesn't actually begin its existence as clutter; pretty much all of it started out as something useful, interesting, attractive, enjoyable.

But in time – over the months and years – the things we've bought or acquired reach a point where they're no longer useful, enjoyable etc. Instead of recognizing that we no longer need or like so many of these things, we build and buy more storage – wardrobes, cupboards and shelves, chests and boxes – to store more and more possessions. As someone once said, 'We're lost in the noise of our own consumption.'

Why do we acquire more than we need?

There are several reasons why we acquire more than we think we need to:

For future use; just in case.   Even if we don't need it now, many of us buy and keep hold of things thinking, 'I might need this some day.'

To improve our lives.   We believe that if we buy this, that or the other, we'll have more fun and be more fun, we'll know more, be better entertained, look better, feel better and so on.

As mementos and souvenirs.   We buy small and relatively inexpensive things; reminders of a place visited, an occasion, an achievement.

We think we need it.   Of course we know that buying things we never use is a waste of money. But so often we don't know if something is unnecessary until after we buy it and it sits in a cupboard, wardrobe, shed etc. untouched for months or even years.

Advertising often encourages us to believe that we 'need' and 'have' to have things. For our clothes, for example, we 'need' a wide range of cleaning products: something for colours and something else to wash our whites; a special liquid for delicates and another one for woollens. Apparently, we also 'need' all sorts of cleaning products to remove dirt and dust, stains and smells in our homes: one for the sink, a separate cleaning product for the loo, another for the bath, one for the shower, one for the bathroom floor, another the kitchen floor and something else for the kitchen counter. Washing-up liquid for the dishes and dishwasher tablets for the dishwasher. Of course, we 'need' a whole other range of products to clean ourselves – soap, wipes, shower gel, cleanser, shampoo etc.

To solve problems. How to slice and dice? Chop and peel? It turns out every known item of food has at least one tool to help you deal with it: a bagel slicer, pizza slicer, pastry cutters, vegetable peeler, garlic press, roast cutting tongs, a rice maker, vegetable steamer and, of course, a knife cleaning clip. The list is endless. But actually there's not much you need in a kitchen to prepare and cook food: some pots and pans, a couple of sharp kitchen knives and a few other tools. What you don't need is a specialized tool to slice your tomatoes, another one for boiled eggs and another one to slice avocados. Do you?

Blogger Katie Berg describes her time living with her partner and children in Nicaragua:

> Side by side, we did the same things as Nicaraguan people – eat, play, learn, travel – but we always needed more stuff to do it. It's easy to say 'that's the difference between rich and poor – having stuff versus not having stuff,' but … the truth is we had fundamentally different ways of problem solving. If we had a need, we'd … search for something to add to our lives – most often that meant shopping. Nicaraguans found

solutions with what they already had. Yes, poverty demands ingenuity to use what's available, but the inverse is not true. Wealth doesn't demand we acquire something new every time we perceive ourselves lacking.

www.skywaymom.com/category/nicaragua/

The stress of it all

All this stuff is proving, in many ways, to be bad for the planet and bad for people. We're facing a clutter crisis.

Some of us know we own too much stuff. Some of us don't. Either way, we feel overwhelmed and burdened by our clutter. Clutter drains our time and energy and takes up space. Drawers don't close, cupboards are jammed full and shelves are filled from top to bottom. We often can't see what to wear for all our clothes.

Physical clutter leads to mental clutter, making it harder to think straight. Clutter competes for your attention; it keeps you aware that there's always something else that needs to be done: to be cleaned, cleared and put away, to be fixed or folded or found. We get frustrated when we can't find something – phones, keys and paperwork – amongst all our stuff. It's disheartening and stressful.

In a nutshell

- Having too much stuff is the new normal. Stuff that takes up space, thought, energy, time or money.
- In the past, material goods were difficult to acquire and were expensive. If you could acquire something, you got it and kept hold of it.

- Now, things are relatively inexpensive and easy to acquire but we're keeping it all; filling our homes and lives without really noticing that it's happening.
- We acquire more things to improve our lives, because we think we 'have' to have them, to help us cope with a situation or just in case we need things in the future.
- Most of our things started out as something useful, interesting, attractive, enjoyable. But in time – over the months and years – the things we've bought or acquired reach a point where they're no longer useful or enjoyable. They're clutter.
- Keeping so many things that served you in the past but no longer serve you today means that you're holding yourself in that past.
- All this stuff is proving, in many ways, to be bad for the planet and bad for people. We're facing a clutter crisis; overwhelmed and burdened by our clutter.

2

Why Can't You
Clear It All Out?

If, then, clutter is a burden – frustrating, disheartening and stressful – why don't we just all have a good clear out? If decluttering is such a good thing, then why is it so hard to do? There are a number of reasons why you, like many of us, might be suffering from declutter paralysis.

Can't get on top of it

Perhaps you can't face a clear out on your own – you blame your partner for not helping or you blame yourself for not having enough time to declutter.

It could be, though, that you've made a start before but you're just not sure what to do with it all, so clutter just moves around the house and never gets tackled effectively. Maybe you give up half-way through because you get bored or irritated with the process; you shove a load of things back into drawers and cupboards only to attempt the whole thing again another time.

Or, you have cleared out the clutter in the past but before long it's the same as it was before. You look around thinking, 'How did this happen? No point spending time and energy on having another clear out, it won't make any real difference, it'll soon mount up again.'

Maybe you think a proper clear out will turn you into a minimalist nightmare: obsessing and nagging others to be neat and tidy.

Hopes and fears

Perhaps, though, you've never really attempted a clear out; you just don't know where to start; you know you've got far more things than you use or really need but you feel overwhelmed by it all. Every item is going to require a decision. What to keep or let go? What to repair? Sell or give things away? Give to friends, family or a charity?

Maybe you worry about making the 'wrong' decision. Even though you haven't needed it in the past year and, in most cases, you could borrow or buy a new one if you really needed to, you ask yourself, 'What if I give it away and then need it in a month, a year or even five years from now?' Or, 'What if I chuck it out and I can never find another one like it? What if I lose weight or gain weight? What if I get ill, lose my job, move home?'

If you're afraid to let go of things, you have 'fear-based' clutter. On the other hand, there are things you might be holding onto out of hope. You hope, for example, to lose weight so you don't want to throw out the clothes you hope you might one day fit into. Or perhaps you hope to catch up on reading, so you keep the books and magazines.

Perhaps you hope that, some day – when you have the time, more money, the children grow up – you'll finish that craft, decorating or garden project, so it would be best to hang onto the things you'll need for that. But actually, instead of motivating you, the items that make up 'hope-based clutter' just serve to remind you of what you still haven't got round to.

Holding onto the past

It seems an inescapable fact of modern life that we learn, define, and remind ourselves of who we are by our possessions.

Russell W. Belk

Maybe what's stopping you from throwing things out is not your fears and hopes about what you might need in the future. Maybe it's about the past.

We identify ourselves by the things around us. Photos, souvenirs and memorabilia remind us of the places we've been and the things we've done in the past. Letting go of things can be like letting go of a part of ourselves.

So many of our possessions have memories attached to them and we don't want to lose those memories. A suit, for example, that you wore in your first job. You loved that job! Never mind that it looks dated, or that you now work in a job where you don't have to wear a suit any more. You know you don't need it but you're unwilling to let go.

Perhaps you feel it's not the right time to let go of some of your things. You have things that, when you look at them, you feel sad to have lost the times, relationships and places

23

those things remind you of, but without the objects to trigger those memories, how would you remember them? You don't want to lose those memories.

If these were someone else's things you would easily identify them as clutter and clear them out. But there's an emotional attachment to many of your things and to the memories that they hold.

Feeling guilty

Attempts to discard things often bring up emotions that are difficult to deal with: sadness, worry, fear, unfulfilled hopes. Avoiding these emotions can be a reason to avoid a clear out. Guilt is a common emotion that gets in the way of a clear out and getting rid of things.

Guilt is a sense that we're doing something 'wrong'. We think things like, 'I can't throw this out because my sister-in-law gave it to me and she'll ask about it if she doesn't see it when she comes over again. It'd be wrong to hurt her feelings.'

Perhaps you think you have something you can't let go of because you've hardly used it or haven't worn it or used it at all. 'I can't give away these clothes, I've never worn them. I can't get rid of these kitchen gadgets, I've hardly used them. I can't chuck out these books – I still haven't read them. It'd be a waste – it'd be wrong.'

It could be that you have family heirlooms – plates, vases, pictures, jewellery – and you think, 'If I don't save them, who will? I feel responsible for them.' Or you tell yourself, 'I can't give this away – my grandmother gave it to me before she died and throwing it away would be wrong; it would look like I don't care about her any more.'

Maybe you're thinking about sunk costs: the time, effort, love or money you have already put in and that you will never get back. The money, for example, you've paid for sports or gym equipment. Or the time and effort you've already put into half-read books or arts and crafts projects. You're embarrassed; you don't want to admit to yourself or anyone else that you were 'wrong' to have bought something in the first place. Anyway, you've kept it for a long time already so might as well hang onto it and continue to live with it. Even though it's plainly not doing you any good.

In a nutshell

- You might be reluctant to clear your clutter because it will take too much time and effort. It may be that you have tried before but never really got on top of it.
- Perhaps you just don't know where to start; you feel overwhelmed by it all. Every item is going to require a decision. What to keep or let go? What if you make the 'wrong' decision? What if you throw out something that you need in future?
- The things you're afraid to let go of make up 'fear-based' clutter. In contrast, 'hope-based' clutter is all the things you hold onto in the hope that some day you'll get round to using, reading, wearing etc.
- Fears and hopes about the future stop us from letting go. So do memories from the past.
- There's an emotional attachment to many of our things and to the memories that they hold. We identify

25

ourselves by the things around us. Letting go of things can be like letting go of a part of ourselves.

- Attempts to discard things often bring up emotions that are difficult to deal with: sadness, worry, fear, unfulfilled hopes. Avoiding these emotions can be a reason to avoid a clear out.
- Guilt – a sense that we're doing something 'wrong' – is a key reason not to let go of so many of our things. We think we're being ungrateful or wasteful if we clear them out.

3
Think Differently

To change skins, evolve into new cycles, I feel one has to learn to discard. If one changes internally, one should not continue to live with the same objects. They reflect one's mind and the psyche of yesterday.

Anais Nin

To clear out clutter successfully requires new ways of thinking and doing. But before you can start *doing* anything, you need to start *thinking* differently. The key to successful decluttering is to change your mindset; to let go of the underlying beliefs and instead take on new, more helpful ways of thinking about things.

When it comes to decluttering, you may have come across the idea of only keeping things that actually bring you joy. Everything else you just get rid of – simple. And it *would* be simple if emotion didn't play a role.

Emotions can complicate the clutter-clearing process. Too often, guilt gets in the way. We keep things because we'd feel guilty if we got rid of them. The things we spent money on and have hardly used or worn. We already feel guilty about that – we don't want to compound the guilt by throwing it out!

But those clothes you've hardly worn, books you never read, toys that are rarely played with, unused kitchen utensils or gym equipment; they're all sunk costs. You've already spent the money. Keeping something you spent £20 or £200 on a while back doesn't bring the money back. The money has gone. So, since you can't get back the time or all the money that you spent on something, it's better only to consider what benefit that thing is to you now.

Whether you've already kept it for a month, year or even half a lifetime, realize that, at the time, you made the right choice; you sincerely thought you *would* wear it, read it, use it. That was then. Holding onto it just ties you to the past. Live in the present!

Changing your mind

Perhaps, though, you think that changing your mind about something implies that you were wrong to buy it in the first place. And being wrong is often seen as a sign of weakness. But whether it's a juicer, gym equipment, a leather jacket or sparkly shoes you no longer want, all that's happened is that you feel differently about it now. That's OK. You're allowed to change your mind! You do it every day, possibly more than you realize. It could've been this morning when you decided to eat toast instead of cereal. You decided to wear a shirt but then you changed your mind and put on a t-shirt. Perhaps it was last night; rather than going out to the pub, you chose to stay in and watch a film instead.

Did you feel guilty about changing your mind? Did you feel you'd done something 'wrong?' It's unlikely. But when it comes to deciding that, actually, you don't want to keep that picture or those candle holders and you don't, after all, need those shot glasses or that spiralizer, you struggle to change course. That bread machine, for example, that you bought so that you could bake bread every day. The reality is no, you are not going to become an artisan baker in the foreseeable future. So let it go; both the fantasy and the bread maker!

That patterned duvet cover from university days in Halls that you've never used since? Know that you loved it then – it served a purpose – but now that time has gone. Instead of feeling guilty about letting go of something, see yourself as flexible and able to adapt.

Think differently about thinking differently; rather than feeling bad about having changed your mind about some of your stuff, feel good; simply see yourself as having made a new decision.

If you can change your mind, you can change your life.

William James

It's the same with the things you no longer want or never liked that were given to you as gifts. Maybe you tell yourself it'd be wrong to throw something out. You don't want to hurt the gift giver's feelings. But your friends and family gave you the gifts to make you happy, not to make you feel guilty, didn't they? Don't let gifts become burdens. Try and separate your feelings about the person from the gift itself; you can still like the person but dislike the gift they gave you.

What about inherited clutter? Have you ever thought, 'They'd be disappointed and upset if they knew I'd let that go. I *have* to hold onto it.' But you're not responsible for other people's clutter. Of course, keep any inherited items you love or find useful, but anything else, if you don't like it, for whatever reason, let it go.

Remember, you're just letting go of the item, you're not letting go of the person or every memory of them.

Of course, we all have things that help us feel connected to a person or occasion and bring back happy memories, but you really don't need a lot of things to remind you of another person or a meaningful time in your life. The embroidered place mats your much-loved great aunt gave you, your children's first pair of shoes, the photos, the pair of champagne glasses from your wedding, the outfits you wore for special occasions; most everything we own has some memory attached to it. We'd never throw anything out if we kept everything because of the memories.

Take a mindful approach; be aware that holding on to so many things just because they remind you of the past encourages you to look back at what was, instead of living more fully in the present and looking forward to the future. Still hanging on to school, college or university assignments? Why? Those days have gone.

You can always keep a few favourite things from the past, just be selective about what you keep to remind you of people, places and experiences.

Rethinking guilt

Still think you'll feel guilty if you clear things out and let them go? Fine. But your guilt is misplaced. As someone once said: guilt is good for you, provided it lasts no longer than five minutes and it brings about a change in behaviour. Like all emotions, guilt has a positive purpose. The purpose of guilt is to prompt you to put right a wrong. When it comes to decluttering, it's helpful to think differently about what you're doing 'wrong'; you refocus the guilt so that it serves you well.

Imagine if someone had something you needed. They could easily give it or sell it to you, but they don't. They never use it themselves, they don't need it and they don't love it. They just hold onto it, never giving you or anyone else an opportunity to make use of it or enjoy it.

When you hold onto something that you don't need, don't use or don't like, you're withholding it from someone who does need it, could use it and/or would love it. And that's not right. *That's* wrong. If you think of it in terms of withholding something that could benefit someone else, that's not legitimate guilt, it's misplaced guilt. So, instead of feeling guilty for letting go of stuff, feel guilty for *not* letting go. Sell it or give it away. If you aren't using it, it is a greater waste to keep it when someone else could use it or enjoy it. So see letting go as an opportunity to benefit someone else.

Whether you give it away or sell it, tell yourself, 'This belongs in someone else's life.' Let someone else use or enjoy the things you no longer use or need.

Organizations like Freecycle aim to keep useful stuff out of landfill. Your things are actually as good as landfill in your home if you are not using them or you don't like them. If anything is unwanted and worthless to you then it's trash, junk, rubbish. Why keep rubbish in your home? Why would you want your home to be as bad as the bin?

One person's trash is another person's treasure. In the past couple of years, through Freecycle (www.freecycle.org), I've given away stuff that myself or my family no longer want, like or need. Lego, for example, that our three sons loved and gave them hours and hours of pleasure; one box of Lego was collected by a woman who sent it to her son working for a children's charity in Rwanda, the other box we gave to someone who took it to a local play centre for children with special needs.

A collection of Simpsons comics went to a chap who told me, 'My son will be so thrilled when he comes home from school to find I've got these for him.' A didgeridoo that was a gift from a friend went to someone who, in his email asking if he could collect it, wrote 'This would make a great addition to my collection of weird and wonderful wooden objects. I would also love to be able to play it one day. That and the banjo, that is.' The young woman who asked for the camera I no longer wanted told me she was going to give it as a gift to a friend.

When I cleared out the shed, a spare pair of wellington boots and a garden chair were picked up by someone who'd recently acquired an allotment. Several children's spades went to a woman whose kids recently lost their spades: they'd been stolen from the park sandpit. The pop-up tent that one son bought for Glastonbury one year was collected by someone else who was off to Glastonbury the following year. The storage heater bricks were collected by a man who was going to make an outdoor pizza oven. Ceramic wall tiles went to an art student who was using them to decorate a table she was making.

In some other cultures, people think differently about their things. For Native Americans of the Northwest Coast, what matters is not what a person has but what they give away to others. 'Giveaway' or 'potlatch', for example, is a custom where people learn to give eagerly because in so doing they reflect the generosity of the many non-human entities that provide for human sustenance. But in European and American culture, which emphasizes property ownership and saving for oneself, giving is seen as a sacrifice, often resulting in feelings of loss or of giving up something.

This type of system appears unbalanced and isolating to Native Americans. For them, passing it on – it can be an item that still has a good potential for use but the person is no longer using it – is a way to honour both the item and the person who will use it now. In fact, it was considered perfectly fine to take back a gift if the gift was not being used by the person it was given to. Not using it was a sign of disrespect. So, they had no qualms about taking back a gift and giving it to someone who would use it.

What if I do need this some day?

Some of us think holding on makes us strong, but sometimes it's letting go.

Herman Hesse

Keeping things because of a sense of guilt or duty, or an inability to let go of the past, is no way to feel in your own home.

Neither is keeping things 'just in case': just in case you run out of money, just in case you lose your job, just in case your relationship breaks down, just in case you move home and so on. Too often we hold onto things in case something bad or unpleasant happens. But rather than feeling reassured by its presence, anything we keep as a result of our 'what if' and 'just in case' thinking only serves to keep us stuck with the worst case scenario that we're worried about.

Live differently – let go of stuff with the knowledge that, in most cases, you could borrow or buy another one if you really needed to. And in the meantime, you haven't had to store it. Let Amazon and eBay, shops, markets and car boot sales and even other people's sheds and garages store those things until the time comes when you need anything you've cleared out. Kitchenware, for example, and every small appliance ever known can be bought cheaply from car boot sales, eBay etc. On one of the days I was writing this book, eBay's auction site had 117 ice-cream makers listed, starting at £2, and 120 bread makers starting at £5.

Top Tip: Write it down. It's not easy to think logically and rationally when you're worried; worrying and problem solving are two very different things. Once you've identified how and where you could access an item again, you may well find it easier to let go of things that you're holding onto 'just in case.'

Take a piece of paper. On the left-hand side of the page, write down each item you're holding onto 'just in case'. On the right-hand side, write down where you could find, borrow or buy it again. Now, when you're finding it difficult to let go of anything, for each object or item, know that you can let go and if you need it again you will already have thought of what to do and where to get it.

Hope-based clutter

Perhaps it's not so much that you're worried you'll need something in the future, it's more that you're *hoping* that some day you'll need it. You tell yourself, 'When I have the time, more energy or money or when my kids grow up or when I lose weight or get fitter I will use/wear it.'

Really? Will you? Are you sure about that? Be honest with yourself. Keeping things around that just remind you of what you're *not* doing is no way to live! Rather than fill you with hope, keeping these things will most likely have the reverse effect. Instead of motivating you, the things that make up 'hope-based clutter' – unused sports equipment, clothes no longer worn, books not read and so on – just serve to remind you of what you still haven't got round to.

Live in the present; free up space in your home for something you need, want or want to do now.

Focus on the benefits

Remember what your house is for. Is it a place for you to enjoy and to live in joyfully? Or is it for you to store items that feel like a crime to get rid of?

Sheila Chandra

Clearing out the clutter is not about leaving you with a minimalist, soulless home – to end up with as little as possible – it's not about that. It's about getting rid of crap so that your home is filled with lovely, useful things. Just like thinning out plants or pruning shrubs, clearing out clutter creates light and room for strong, new growth.

Whatever it is that you're holding onto, ask yourself why. Identify and acknowledge the feelings and emotions that arise. Then decide what you have to gain by clearing your clutter; focus on the benefits.

How might your life be better with less stuff? Which of these potential benefits appeals to you?

- Clearing clutter takes time but, once it's done properly, it takes far less time and effort to keep it that way.
- Having less stuff means you have less to keep clean, organized and put away. It will be much quicker and easier to keep your home clean and tidy.
- Clutter competes for your attention; everywhere you look you see something that needs to be cleared and put away or that needs to be fixed or folded or whatever. It's much easier to manage and take care of just a few things.
- You'll be able to think more clearly. You'll feel less stressed, less frustrated.
- You'll have calm, organized spaces that support how you would like to live in your home.
- You'll need fewer cupboards, shelves, drawers, chests, bags and boxes to store things, so there'll be more clear space in each room.
- You'll be surrounded only by things you like and need. You won't have things that, although you feel you 'should' hold onto them, you don't actually like. You'll end up with a home in which the majority of items are things you truly love or that are useful in some way.
- You'll feel so much lighter and more in control of your stuff rather than feeling like it's controlling you. You'll learn to be less attached to possessions.
- No longer will you have to hunt through a drawer full of paperwork, scrabble around in a kitchen drawer for the right utensil, or root through hanger after hanger of clothes for what you want to wear that day.
- You'll always know where to find things. You'll spend less time looking for the things you need because you

actually know where they are. Everything has a place and you know exactly where to find everything.

- Things are easier to put away after you've used them. No longer will you be trying to jam or stuff things back into drawers, cupboards or your wardrobe.
- You could make money. All that stuff you've got; some of it could be turned into hard cash. Money to spend on – not necessarily more possessions – but things like a meal out with friends, a day out, maybe even a weekend away.
- When you let go of the things you don't use, want or like, you are doing good; someone else will benefit from your giving.

Top Tip: *Think positive. Think about what you have to gain rather than what you have to lose by letting go of things. Whatever you identify as the benefits of clearing out your clutter, keep in mind the good reasons. Write them down and pin them up where you can see them every day as a reminder to help motivate you.*

In a nutshell

- Clearing clutter requires new ways of thinking and doing. But before you can start *doing* anything, you need to start *thinking* differently; to take on new, more helpful ways of thinking about things.
- If you've acquired something you've hardly or never used, realize that, at the time, you made the right choice; you sincerely thought you *would* wear it, read it or use it. That was then. Keeping it just ties you to the past. Live in the present!

- Take a mindful approach; be aware that holding onto so many things just because they remind you of the past encourages you to look back at what was, instead of living more fully in the present and looking forward to the future.
- You can always keep a few favourite things from the past, just be selective about what you keep to remind you of people, places and experiences.
- Think differently about thinking differently; rather than feeling bad about having changed your mind and no longer wanting some of your possessions, feel good – see yourself as having made a new decision.
- Don't let gifts become burdens. Try and separate your feelings about the person from the gift itself; you can still like the person but dislike the gift they gave you.
- When you hold onto something that you don't need, don't use or don't like, you're withholding it from someone who does need it, could use it and/or would love it. If you aren't using it, it is a greater waste to keep it when someone else could use it or enjoy it. See letting go as an opportunity to benefit someone else.
- Rather than feeling assured by its presence, 'fear-based' clutter – the things you keep as a result of 'what if' and 'just in case' thinking – only serves to keep you stuck with the worst case scenario that you're worried about.
- Let go of things with the knowledge that, in most cases, you could borrow or buy another one if you really needed to.
- Hope-based clutter – unused sports equipment, clothes no longer worn, books not read and so on – just serves to remind you of what you still haven't got round to

doing, reading, wearing etc. Live in the present; free up space in your home for something you need, want or want to do now.

- Whatever it is that you're holding onto, ask yourself why. Identify and acknowledge the feelings and emotions that arise. Then focus on what you have to gain by clearing your clutter; focus on the benefits.

4
Declutter Your Home

No one lets go without reaching for something else.

Julie Morgenstern

What, then, do you think you will gain by clearing your clutter? How might your life be better with less stuff? What have you decided you want to achieve? What are you aiming for?

Perhaps it's the idea of freeing yourself from things you don't actually like or need that appeals to you; your aim is only to have things in your home that you need or love. Or maybe it's the thought of more space and less stuff to keep clean, organize and put away that most appeals to you; no longer will you be trying to jam or stuff things back into drawers, cupboards or your wardrobe. Maybe you simply want to clear all that clutter so that, in future, everything has a place and you'll know exactly where to find everything.

Whatever it is, once you start decluttering, having a clearly defined reason or reasons will help to keep you focused and motivated. You'll have something specific to aim for: an overall goal, intention or vision. Next, you can move onto identifying your objectives: the individual steps you'll need to take – the specific tasks – in order to achieve your aim.

Think it through

It's not enough just to think, 'I want to declutter my home.' Or, 'I want less stuff and more space.' How will you do it? What will it involve? If, for example, your aim was to have more space in your bedroom, then your first step – your first objective – might be to sort out your bedroom wardrobe. Break that down even further and the first, smaller step might be to sort through all the pairs of trousers you own. The next step could be to go through your shirts and then your shoes. Once the wardrobe is sorted, the next step of your aim to declutter your bedroom might be to clear out a chest of drawers, one drawer at a time.

Identify the steps you need to take and think through how you will do them. Breaking the task down into smaller steps will make it feel more manageable and less overwhelming. You'll have a path to follow: a guide. It's easier to get straight on to the next step if you have already thought about what it will be. It allows you to keep the pace going.

Top Tip: Write it down. Rather than let your thoughts about how you'll tackle decluttering – the steps you'll take – stay in your head and clutter your mind, you might find it helpful to write them down. Writing down your ideas can help you decide where to start and give you direction and focus.

Make decision making easier

In any one day, you can be faced with many decisions: what to wear, what to eat, where to eat, where to go, how to get there, what time to come and go, who to talk to, who not to talk to, who to email, what to watch, what to listen to and so on. Individually, most of these decisions are fairly straight-forward. But, all together, in any one day they add up exponentially – at a steady and often rapid rate. They clutter your mind!

Your brain can only make a certain number of decisions before it reaches 'decision fatigue.' When he was US President, Barack Obama had a method for making decision making as simple as possible. Issues requiring a decision from the President were submitted in writing (known as 'decision memos') with three check-boxes at the bottom: 'agree', 'disagree' and 'let's discuss'. Of course, the issues would have been important – why else would they end up at the desk of the President – but creating so few choices simplified and sped up the decision making. 'You need to focus your decision-making energy,' he said in a magazine interview, 'You need to routinize yourself.'

Get more presidential about *your* decision-making!

Keep or don't keep

The most simple approach is to decide whether you keep or don't keep each item. If you don't like it or love it or need it, let it go. Anything in your home that you look at and don't like, that makes you feel sad or guilty – it goes.

If you need it, like it or love it – it stays.

Pros: For each item, you only have one decision to make each time.

Cons: You have to be prepared to be ruthless. You may spend too much time agonizing over some items; whether to keep or not.

Keep. Maybe keep. Don't keep

With this approach, you declutter in two stages. First you go through things and decide what you definitely do want, don't want and maybe want. Then you go back over the 'maybe' things that you've put aside and decide what to definitely keep and what to let go of.

Pros: Rather than agonize over, 'Shall I keep it or let it go?' with every item, the 'maybe' can be gone through the next time. And the next time you go back to each item in the maybe pile, it's often clearer whether or not to keep it.

Cons: Too much in the 'maybe keep' pile might mean it never gets cleared out.

Top Tip: If you are still not sure whether you can definitely get rid of something, put it in a box. Then store the box somewhere out of the way. Put a note on your calendar six months from now to look in the box. Then pull it out, six months later, and see if it's anything you really needed.

Beginner's mind and acceptance and commitment

There are two aspects of mindfulness that can help with deciding what to keep and not keep. One is a concept known as 'beginner's mind', and the other is 'acceptance and commitment'.

With a 'beginner's mind', rather than let the past influence what you hold onto, you let the present guide you. So, for each thing – object, item, piece of clothing etc. – you can't decide whether to keep or not, ask yourself, 'If today was the first time I'd seen it – would I buy it now?'

The second mindfulness concept is 'acceptance and commitment'. What this means is that, instead of trying to battle with memories, thoughts and feelings, you acknowledge the memories and accept how you feel about something – that it was once useful, that you liked or loved it.

For example, you might say to yourself, 'I remember when/ where I bought this. That was such a good holiday.' Or, 'This was so useful for me all those years ago.' Or, ' I had so much fun with this.' And then let it go.

Simply say to yourself, 'I'm sad to let it go.' Or, 'I don't need/like it any more.' Recognize when something that was once useful, liked or loved has evolved into clutter and then turn your attention to what you've committed to – to declutter – and let it go.

Clutter-clearing actually gives you the chance to relive fond memories, while putting your things in order. You'll learn to be less attached to possessions.

Top Tip: Write your thoughts about it. Acknowledge the memories, hopes and emotions that can arise with each item. What does the item represent to you? What memories are attached to that item?

Get started

So you know you need to have a clear out but you don't know if you'll have the time or energy?

Is it because you just can't be bothered? Or perhaps you're perfectionist – and unless you can do it perfectly, you won't do it at all?

Maybe you have a vision in your mind of what, ideally, you want a room to look like. If you're going to declutter, you have to do everything: a big clear out, move furniture, sort through every single thing, clean and reorganize what you keep. It would take up all of your weekend. And as you rarely have a whole weekend free, to declutter and clean, knowing that you won't be able to do the room perfectly, you just don't do it.

But there's no need to wait for the day when you'll have the time, money and energy to devote to clearing, cleaning and sorting. Get started now and even if you can't create that ideal room that you have in mind, you can apply your perfectionism to each drawer, shelf, cupboard etc.

Deadlines

It took time to get all that stuff; it'll take some time to clear it out. Deciding how much you want to declutter and by when can be the push you need to get started and keep going on the decluttering process. You might decide, for example, that you want to have decluttered the living room by Christmas. Or that you're going to sort out the kitchen before your birthday party next month. Knowing when you want to achieve something helps focus your efforts. Without a deadline, there's nothing to motivate you to get on with it. It's easy to make excuses and put off having a clear out because there's no pressure; nothing to compel you to get started and keep going.

However, although deadlines can be positive and motivate you, the pressure can be stressful. If you don't meet the deadline or reach your target, you risk feeling like you've failed and that you might as well give up. So, if you think giving yourself a deadline to reach is unhelpful, simply focus on working consistently towards what it is you want to achieve, one step at a time. Establish realistic expectations for yourself. Declutter in small, focused bursts; make each decluttering session a hill to climb, not a mountain! Work in the way you prefer, and what you feel comfortable with given the time you have available.

No matter how many mistakes you make or how slow you progress, you're still way ahead of anyone who isn't trying.

Tony Robbins

Set yourself up for success

You can do it! It may not be easy, and it may not be able to be done in a week, but it is possible. Yes, the idea of sorting through and clearing out your stuff can feel daunting. But you're not going to do it all in one go. You'll be breaking it down into smaller, more doable pieces of work, focusing on one area at a time. Just as clutter arises gradually over time, so it can take time to deal with it.

Even if you have the time and energy to declutter all in one go, you are still going to have to do it one step at a time: one cupboard, one collection, one room after another.

Whether you spend an hour once a week decluttering or do half an hour every day, it doesn't really matter. Because *any* time that you devote to the process moves you one step closer to a clearer, calmer home.

Simply making a start creates the momentum needed. Take Jo, for example. Jo works full time and is a parent of two teenagers. 'On a weekend, it'd start with me intending to sort through and clear out more of my stuff and things the boys no longer used,' she says. 'But each time, despite my good intentions, I just couldn't face it; I didn't *feel* like doing it. However, even though I didn't feel like sorting through things, I'd just make a start. Before I knew it, I'd be absorbed. What gets me started is knowing that I will feel like decluttering if I just get started.'

Like Jo, don't expect to feel like it before you do anything. Instead, expect that it's normal *not* to feel like it in the beginning and be prepared to move through that reluctant feeling on your way to sorting things out and achieving a clutter-free environment. Get started and, quite soon, the momentum will take over and you'll find yourself easily carrying on with what you intended to do. All it takes is a little effort at the start.

Not sure if you can do it? Make a deal with yourself: tell yourself you'll do it for, say, just 10 minutes, or 20 or 30 minutes. Instead of trying to clear the entire kitchen, for example, tell yourself you'll just do it for 10 minutes; one drawer, say. You may well find that once you get going, you end up continuing well past the 10-minute mark you'd decided on.

Decide what is the one thing you could do first. Then do that one thing. Give it your full attention. Just clear out one drawer.

This approach – committing to a short amount of time – is known as 'acting as if'. You approach the task *as if* you want to do it. You don't have to wait for your thoughts and feelings to change before you get going. You get going 'as if' you actually want to and your feelings will change. Once you get going, if you have a plan for the steps you need to take and you have simple categories for deciding what to do with each item – keep, don't keep – it makes it easier to move on from one thing to the next.

Having a time limit for each decluttering session can help prevent you from being distracted.

If, for example, you find yourself reading passages from books when you intended to be sorting them out, knowing you only have a certain amount of time – 10 minutes, 30 minutes, an hour or whatever – can keep you focused.

Top Tip: If you have a hard time getting started, imagine you are encouraging a friend who is trying to clear their clutter. Then tell yourself those positive words. Try phrases such as, 'I can do this,' 'I can take my time,' or, 'This is so going to be worth it; I'm going to have a home that only has the things I need, really like or love.'

Start with the easy stuff

Start with the easiest decisions you can. Start with the easy stuff and you'll feel like you're getting somewhere; that you're making progress quite quickly and then you'll feel encouraged to continue the next day or whenever the next time is.

Start with:

- A room, an area, a cupboard, collection etc. that's irritating you the most.
- Somewhere where you'll notice a big difference. The wardrobe that you can longer fit any more clothes

in – start there. The drawer that you have to push and shove to close because it's so full – start there.

- A visible area or place where you'll see results quickly – open shelves, for example.
- A room that's most used, such as the kitchen.
- Things that don't come with emotional attachments. Too many things in the bathroom – start there.

Starting with some quick wins can really help get you motivated to continue and to tackle more. How else can you identify the easy stuff? It's the stuff you definitely want to keep. Or the stuff you definitely don't want. How do you know? You definitely want to keep it if you:

- Need it: it's useful and you use it regularly.
- Love it: it's beautiful, you enjoy it, it makes you happy.
- Have to have it: for legal reasons/records.

You definitely don't want to keep it if you:

- Don't need it or have to have it: it's no longer useful or it's broken or outdated.
- Don't like it: it makes you feel irritated, annoyed or stressed.

Top Tip: Start by getting 10 items in your home that you already know you need, want or love – then gauge all other decisions against those.

The first step

The first step in every declutter is pulling everything out so you can see what you have. If it's a drawer or shelf, simply empty it on a table. If you know you keep more of one thing in more than one room – books, coats and jackets, paper-work, games etc. – then when you're in one room, collect them from the other rooms too. This way you can see and assess everything you've got in that group all in one go.

Top Tip: You might find it helpful to take everything out of the room it's kept in. Sometimes being in a different room from the one in which you're used to seeing your things can help you be more objective about it.

Bathroom

Get all of your lotions, potions, makeup, shampoo and other products. Put the things you regularly use – use every day or every week – back where they belong. Throw out the rest. The same goes for cleaning products.

If you keep medications in the bathroom, clear out medicines that are no longer needed or out of date. Don't throw meds in the bin, down the sink or loo, instead they should be taken to your local pharmacy for safe disposal.

Kitchen

Plates, mugs, dishes, pots, pans and utensils you use every day, keep, of course. But it's possible that they've been cloning them-selves while you weren't looking. How many knives, pots, pans, wooden spoons, plates, glasses etc. do you really need?

If you have crockery you love, use it every day. If it is stuck in a box somewhere and you never use it, give it to someone who will.

Any number of mugs and glasses over the total number of people you would ever have drinking in your home at any one time – chuck them out. Unless you have large parties often, you don't need 30 wine glasses. If you only have large gatherings once every few years, it would make more sense to ask friends to bring extra glasses or hire them.

Pans you don't use, dishes you don't like, chipped, stained crockery and plastic storage containers without lids – get rid of them. If you never bake, you don't need cupcake tins cluttering your cupboards. Chuck them out. Plastic food containers should have corresponding lids. If you don't have one or the other, throw it out.

Kitchen equipment – do you have a bread maker, liquidizer, juicer, spiralizer or food processor that's too much trouble to use, so you don't use it? With each item, ask yourself, 'When did I last use this item?' A year ago? Never? Out it goes.

Top Tip: Ask yourself, 'If I was out shopping right now, would I buy this?' Or, 'If I lent this to someone and they didn't return it, would I really care'?

Top Tip: When you put things back, don't fill up each cupboard, drawer or shelf. Aim to leave space so that you can see and reach things more easily.

Clear the worktops – kitchen counters are for preparing food, not stacking up bottles of seasonings and oils. If things don't have a home, your kitchen counter becomes home for everything.

Dump anything that's out of date: packets, tins and jars. Check to see if it's too ancient to eat or if you just don't want it any more. Anything that's still good but you'll never eat, you could give to a food bank. (Always check with your local foodbank before donating to see what supplies they are currently in need of.)

Get everything out of the fridge and the freezer. Put back anything you'll eat in the next month; use or chuck out anything else.

Collections

Trophies, ornaments, vinyl records, antique spoons, action superman models, stamps, seashells, paperweights, glassware, and books, books, books.

Are you still adding to your collection? Is the collection on display? Are the items in use? If your collection is taking up too much space and too much time and it feels like none of it is special, attractive to you or used by you, then it's clutter. If you're just accumulating more and more for your collection and it's just piling up, it's clutter. If a collection makes you happy, then it's not clutter. You *can* have a clutter-free lifestyle and still have collections. There just needs to be a place to keep and/or display the collection.

Be a curator not a collector. A curator is a person who selects the best examples of something for presentation, rather than just acquiring and keeping things for the sake of having lots of something; evaluate and edit.

Choose quality over quantity. Show off your treasures. Choose what you are going to display. Some things are born to be displayed: antique glass, beautiful books and pictures.

Top Tip: Google 'How to display your collections' for some creative, inspiring ideas.

Decide where you're going to keep your collection. When the shelf/box/cupboard is full, you stop adding. If you acquire a new item, you must let go of another one from the collection. Your collection becomes refined without the hoarder aspect.

Decide that you'll only keep, for example, 20 of your most recent or 20 of your favourite items from a collection. Or that, for example, you'll use only three of your bookcase shelves for displaying a collection.

Once your limit is reached, use the 'one in, one out' rule. That way, you can keep on enjoying the fun of collecting.

Janine has an elephant collection. She explains, 'There are three ceramic elephants grouped on a bookshelf in the living room. I've got a jade elephant in my bathroom, a painting of an elephant in the hall and a fantastic black and white photo in my bedroom. They're all part of the same collection, and they all look great where they are. A collection doesn't have to be lots and lots of one thing – a hoard – all together cluttering up one shelf; it can be a single thing here, another thing there.'

Make sure you always have some room to grow your collection. Leave some space so you can keep on enjoying collecting without having to expand the space allotted to your collection. Set boundaries, either in number or space.

What's the difference between hoarding and collecting?

The NHS website (www.nhs.uk/Conditions/hoarding/) explains, 'Many people collect items such as books or stamps and this isn't considered a problem. The difference between a "hoard" and a "collection" is how these items are organized.

'A collection is usually well ordered and the items are easily accessible. A hoard is usually very disorganized, takes up a lot of room and the items are largely inaccessible.

'For example, someone who collects newspaper reviews may cut out the reviews they want and organize them in a catalogue or scrapbook. Someone who hoards may keep large stacks of newspapers that clutter their entire house and mean it's not actually possible to read any of the reviews they wanted to keep.

'Someone who has a hoarding disorder may typically:

- Keep or collect items that may have little or no monetary value, such as junk mail and carrier bags, or items they intend to reuse or repair.
- Find it hard to categorize or organize items.'

Top Tip: Enlist a friend. It could be a friend who will challenge you and ask questions: 'Are you really going to repair those bikes? What on earth are you still doing with all those cheap perfumed candles?' Or encourages and supports you to let go of sentimental things. It could be a friend who simply makes the process much more fun.

Maybe you know someone else who's also feeling over-whelmed by how much stuff they have. You could serve as a source of support for one another. You might decide to work together, taking turns helping one another. Or you might declutter separately but take before and after photos to text each other.

Clothes

T-shirts and shirts, suits, coats and jackets, trousers, skirts and dresses, work clothes, weekend clothes, sports clothes, shoes, boots and bags, hats, scarves and belts – all those clothes! You probably can't see what to wear for all your clothes. Most of us have too many and most of us wear 20% of our clothes 80% of the time.

Sure, a particular t-shirt reminds you of a festival or a pair of shoes brings back memories of the miles you walked sight-seeing during a weekend in Paris, but if you haven't worn something in a year, why have you still got it? And what about something you don't ever feel completely comfortable in? You'll avoid it and always choose something else to wear, effectively allowing it just to take up room in a wardrobe or a drawer.

As for accessories, left to their own devices they seem to multiply. However, there's a limit to how many scarves you need, or how much space you need devoted to belts, hats and gloves.

But how do you choose what to keep and what to get rid of? The two most basic questions to ask are, of course: Do I love it? Do I need it?

Other questions you might want to ask yourself are:

- Do I feel good when I wear it?
- Do I look good when I wear it?
- Am I comfortable in it?
- Is it out of fashion and not coming back? And even if it did, would I probably want the updated version?
- Has my lifestyle changed? Maybe you used to work in an office but now work freelance from home, so you don't need 'office clothes'.
- Does it hold any sentimental attachment?
- Does it need cleaning or mending?

Any things you keep should be items you love, which fit you, are comfortable and suit you.

Top Tip: Use the clothes hanger principle – hang all your clothes facing one direction. As you wear and wash them, flip the hangers. At the end of 6 months, anything hanging the wrong way that obviously hasn't been worn in 6 months, you clear out. You could easily do the same thing with books or records or other items from a collection.

Books

In his autobiographical novel *The Private Papers of Henry Ryecroft,* the 19th-century writer George Gissing wrote, 'There were books of which I had passionate need ... books more necessary to me than bodily nourishment. I could see them, of course, at the British Museum, but that was not at all the same thing as having and holding them – to have and to hold – my own property, on my own shelf.'

More recently, the interior decorator Rita Konig has written, 'I don't think there can be much of an argument against the idea that books really do make a room. In a mix of colours, sizes and patterns, their spines add so much depth and colour to a space.'

For many of us, a house just isn't a home without books. But it doesn't take long for a collection of books to become a mountain: bookcases double-stacked with fiction, biographies, art and design, travel books and history books; recipe books in the kitchen, humour books in the loo; piles of books building up next to the sofa and by your bed.

It's time to pare down your books! Time to pick out those books that you just don't need any more; outdated reference books, old textbooks and books relating to a long-abandoned hobby. Novels you'll never read again and recipe books you never use.

Top Tip: Change the way you think about books – read them and give them away, like magazines.

No doubt, with some books, you feel a connection to the story or particular characters. You'll remember when and where you read particular books. You didn't acquire those books overnight, so you will not release your attachment to them quickly either.

Keep books you really love; those that are worth something, those that you'll reread and are glossy books you'll look through again. But all those paperback novels and outdated reference books you will never read again – they can go.

Start by taking all the books off the shelf. This might seem like a waste of time and effort if you're only going to put them back again, but part of the process involves cleaning the shelves and dusting the books you're going to keep. Books, like most collections of things you love, need to be looked after.

Top Tip: Have a 'desert island' shelf. These are your very favourite books; the books you'd want with you if you were stuck on a desert island, that you could read or look at many times. As you come across these books, add them to your shelf. It can only hold one row of books, no double stacks or piles. Not only is it comforting to know you are definitely keeping those books as you clear out others, you have a physical limit: you can have no more 'desert island' books than will fit in this one space, so you have to think carefully and strategically about your collection.

Photos

Photos represent so many memories, experiences, people and feelings. Photos depict your past; your history. Each photo is a record of people, the friends and family members, places and occasions, achievements and experiences, the fun times, the parties, the laughing, the day trips. But not only do boxes or albums of printed photos take up space, it's hard to enjoy your favourites when they're buried amongst so many other photos that really have no significance and don't help tell a story.

Just like anything else you declutter, sorting and saving the key memories, and getting rid of the ones you don't want, will leave you with only the best ones.

Go through your photos and let go of any that you don't really love. They could be of people you don't remember, people you don't want to remember, places that no longer mean anything to you, blurred pictures, etc. Aim to eliminate 70% of your prints.

Top Tip: Ask yourself, 'If I had to, would I pay to reprint it?' If the answer is no, let it go.

Just as with other sentimental items, search for the treasures and let go of the rest. You'll enjoy so much more being able to look through the most meaningful photos and share the memories and stories, rather than being overwhelmed with packets, boxes and albums full of photos.

Take your time with decluttering photos. There will be lots of memories. But keep in mind the aim of wanting to more easily access and enjoy your photos once you're done.

Consider how they'll be stored, how you'll protect them so they last a long time, how much space they take up, etc. Or maybe you want to declutter them and then scan or take photographs of the ones you keep so you have digital copies.

And when it comes to digital photos, we all take far more photos than we actually need. The convenience of smart-phones, tablets and digital cameras allows us to regularly take dozens of photos, yet nobody wants to sit and look through hundreds of images. Even though these pictures are digital and don't take up a lot of physical space in your home, they can take up a lot of space on your phone. Any time you've got a few minutes (waiting in a line, at an appoint-ment, before a meeting, etc.) just scroll through your phone and delete any you don't want. Every little bit helps.

Home office

Do you have a home office? Start with your desk. If things don't have a home, your desk becomes a home for everything. Start by thinking about what you actually need at your desk, and what can go. As you go through the cupboards and drawers, ask yourself: does this item have a purpose? Is it redundant or outdated? Are you keeping it because you need it, or because you might need it? Did you even remember it was there?

Your bag

How much do you carry around with you every day? What do you load up with before you leave your home? What's in your bag, rucksack or handbag? Are you carrying around stuff 'just in case' – extra pens, notebook, tissues, wipes, safety pins, chewing gum, snacks and so on? Each item we carry around is a little burden, and these little burdens add up. Clear out the clutter.

Paperwork

Are you on top of your paperwork? Or do you have piles of papers: bills, letters to answer, forms to complete, papers to file, contracts, paid invoices, vehicle documents, insurance documents, financial statements, warranties, manuals and instruction leaflets?

You can get them under control! Go through your home and bring all the papers into one place. Put them into one large pile, roll up your sleeves and get busy.

Go through them one at a time, and do one of three things: trash them, file them immediately or put them in an action file. Don't put anything else back on the original pile; don't put them anywhere but in a folder or in the recycling bin.

In general, keep the last 12 months' worth of bills, statements and accounts and keep the most recent version of insurance policies and contracts.

Keep papers you may need to refer back to later or to provide when applying for a job, loan or credit. You should keep legal documents: birth certificates, marriage certificate, divorce papers, passport, deeds, lease agreement, vehicle documents and wills. You should also hang on to medical papers, and receipts for major purchases (for warranty and insurance purposes).

Pick up each paper or document and ask yourself:

- Do I need or have to keep this?
- Is it out of date?
- Can I get the information online?

Top Tip: Manuals and instruction leaflets – check if you can find the instructions on the internet and, if you can, chuck out the hard copies.

You're going to need something to store the papers you need to keep. Depending on how much paperwork you have, use clear plastic sleeves or a folder for each type of record. Then store in a box, an archive box or a collapsible concertina file.

Garden

Outdoor spaces can just as easily become cluttered with unused tools, outdoor furniture, broken pots and plants that, unless you can spend the time and energy nurturing them back to their full glory, are past their best.

Clear out any outhouses, garages, sheds and greenhouses. Simply ask yourself, 'Is it beautiful or useful?' If the answer is no, get rid of it. Get rid of any outdoor toys and equipment your children no longer play with.

Clearing out other people's things

'It's not just me – it's the people I live with. They have so much stuff and it's cluttering up the place.' That may be true; living with other people and their stuff can be frustrating and discouraging. But you can't change someone, or force them to declutter; no point beseeching, berating, criticizing or threatening.

Uncluttering someone else's stuff without permission is not a good idea. No one likes to think that their things are going to disappear because someone else decided their stuff looks like junk or is worthless or unimportant.

Rather than getting rid of your partner's things behind their back, ask if you can go through them and identify those items that seem like good candidates for throwing out, giving away or selling, and then check to see if they agree.

If your partner or housemate refuses to join you in decluttering, work out a compromise. You can still have areas that are yours – your wardrobe or your bedroom – that you have more control over. The living room and kitchen, for example, might be theirs while the home office and bedroom are yours. Each of you is free to do with it what you want: declutter or not. It's up to each person.

Ask if they'll keep their clutter in cupboards, boxes etc. Then your concern is just about them leaving things around the house. If you don't like it, you'll need to clear up after them. If you can live with it, then don't.

Toys

In 2010, UK toy manufacturers Dream Town commissioned research to find out what toys children owned and played with. The research revealed that the average 10-year-old owns 238 toys. But parents reported that their children play with just 12 favourites – just 5% of their toys – on a daily basis. Parents suggested that their children end up picking the same toys, day in and day out, because they have too many to choose from.

How do you help children minimize their stuff without doing it for them? When it comes to decluttering your children's toys you do need to involve them. Everyone should have a choice about their own belongings, even small children. It might be fine for you to throw away a broken toy no one plays with anyway or to give away clothes they've outgrown. For other things, though, involve children in the decision-making process and help them to make decisions about which toys should stay and which should go. What do they play with? What do they love?

Removing toys that they've outgrown and so are no longer using is an easy place to start. And let go of the things they never liked that much, even if *you* loved it or it was a present.

(With children's artwork, at the end of the term, pick the best two or three pieces to keep. At the end of the school year – after three terms – pick out the best two or three.)

If they have a huge collection of toy cars and vehicles, maybe they could clear out at least half of that collection? The zoo of cuddly toy animals? Tell them they can choose, for example, six to ten favourites.

You can train young children to clear up and keep their rooms tidy but don't expect too much from teenagers' bedrooms. Hygiene is important – clothes and dishes need to come out of their rooms to be cleaned – but other than that, leave well alone. They're really not bothered if their clutter and untidiness annoy you. Choose your battles; let it go. Otherwise, your teen will have identified it as a great way to defy you and wind you up. Just insist that their clutter doesn't overflow into the rest of your home.

Ten more things to clear out of your home

- Most of what's in the loft!
- Excess furniture.
- Any decorating/DIY supplies that you no longer need.
- Old or broken exercise or sports equipment.
- Bed linen you never use.
- Towels and table cloths you no longer use.
- Jewellery that you don't wear.
- DVDs and CDs.
- Old phones, computers, chargers for phones you no longer own.
- Abandoned art and craft and other projects and their accompanying tools and materials.

Of course, this chapter hasn't covered everything – every room and every type of object and item – you might have in your home. But now you can go through the rest of your home – the hallway, the living room, the understairs cupboard, the conservatory, the garage – using the same methods and principles.

Reflect on your achievements – even the small ones!

What to do with it all

It can really help, as part of your planning, if you know what the options are for what you'll do with the stuff you're going to clear out. Once you've decluttered, you need to get all that stuff out the door. Fast!

Sell it
Ebay. www.ebay.co.uk
Gumtree. www.gumtree.com
Webuybooks. (and CD's, DVD's and games) www.webuybooks. co.uk
Buymywardrobe. Buy and sell preloved, designer fashion. buymywardrobe.com

Give it away
Freecycle. To give away a wide range of things in your town or neighbourhood. www.freecycle.org
Alzheimers Society Old Jewellery Appeal. If you have jewellery that is either broken or no longer wanted, Alzheimer's Society can put it to worthy use by recycling it to raise funds https:// www.alzheimers.org.uk/info/20014/make_a_donation/ 164/donate_old_jewellery

Furniture Re Use Network. Donate furniture or electrical appliances to the Furniture Re-Use Network which helps low-income households. frn.org.uk

Poverty Child. Turns your unwanted stuff into cash for their projects. Coins, UK or foreign currency of any age, bank-notes, coins, stamps, mobile phones, video cameras, old film cameras, digital cameras, sat navs, game consoles, mp3 players, laptops, tablets, jewellery, unwanted gold and silver including damaged items, costume jewellery, and watches. https://povertychild.org/donate-your-old-stuff/?gclid= CKHil7vc4NMCFYWc7Qod3lMOYg

Traidcraft. Turns your unwanted stuff to cash for their projects. Helps change the future for families in the world's poorest communities. Ink cartridges, jewellery and currency. http://www.traidcraft.co.uk/recycling

Note: Poverty Child, Alzheimers Society and Traidcraft all provide Freepost recycling envelopes.

The Trussell Trust. For food donations to a network of food-banks. The Trussell Trust provides emergency food and support to people in crisis. www.trusselltrust.org

Museums. My 1984 Laura Ashley wedding dress was recently accepted by Worthing Museum in West Sussex. It has one of the largest costume collections in the country. http://www.worthingmuseum.co.uk/

The Keep. Collections comprise of important 20th and 21st-century literary, political and social history archives. Family papers and diaries, the records of clubs and societies, an old apprenticeship record, farming and business records, old title deeds; if you think what you have may be of interest, not just for now but in the future, get in touch. www.thekeep.info/donors-and-depositors/

Fix it

Rather than throw it away get a broken item fixed, mended or repaired; Google the manufacturer or look for a YouTube video that will show you how to fix it yourself.

Borrow, hire and lend

Streetbank. Enables neighbours to share anything and everything with each other from tools and instruments to cool boxes and sofa beds. www.streetbank.com

ReadItSwapIt. Swap books you've read for ones you haven't. www.readitswapit.co.uk

In a nutshell

- Having a clearly defined reason for clearing your clutter will help to keep you focused and motivated; you'll have something specific to aim for.
- Breaking the task down into smaller steps will make it less overwhelming. It's easier to get straight on to the next step if you have already thought about what it will be.
- Your brain can only make a certain number of decisions before it reaches 'decision fatigue'. The most simple approach is to ask yourself, 'Do I love it? Do I need it?'
- Not sure? Then have three categories – Keep, Maybe Keep and Don't Keep. First, you go through things and decide what you definitely do want, don't want and maybe want. Then, you go back over the 'maybe' things and decide what to definitely keep and what to let go of.

- Adopt a 'beginner's mind' – rather than let the past influence what you hold onto, let the present guide you. So, for each thing you can't decide whether to keep or not, ask yourself if today was the first time you'd seen it – would you buy it now?
- Take an 'acceptance and commitment' approach: acknowledge the memories and accept how you feel about something – that it was once useful, that you liked or loved it. Then commit to the 'don't keep' pile.
- Set realistic expectations for yourself. Deadlines can motivate you, but the pressure can be stressful. So, instead, focus on working consistently towards what it is you want to achieve, one step at a time.
- Expect that it's normal not to feel like it at the beginning of a clutter-clearing session and be prepared to move through that reluctant feeling on your way to a clutter-free home.
- Get started and, quite soon, the momentum takes over and you may well find yourself easily carrying on. All it takes is a little effort at the start.
- Start with the easiest decisions you can. Start with the easy stuff and you'll feel like you're getting somewhere; quick wins can really help get you motivated to continue and to tackle more.
- Other people's stuff driving you mad? Rather than sneaking out their things, ask if you can go through them and identify those items that don't seem worth keeping and then check to see if they agree.
- If your partner or housemate refuses to join you in decluttering, work out a compromise. You can still have areas that are yours – your wardrobe or your bedroom – that you have more control over.

- Everyone should have a choice about their own belongings, even small children. Involve them and help them to make decisions about which toys should stay and which should go. What do they play with? What do they love?
- Once you've decluttered, you need to get all that stuff out the door. Fast! It can really help, as part of your planning, if you know what the options are for what you'll do with the stuff you're going to clear out.

5
Keep Your Home Free Of Clutter

Once you learn to choose your belongings properly, you will be left only with the amount that fits perfectly in the space you currently own. This is the true magic of tidying.

Marie Kondo

You've cleared the clutter. You're only keeping the things that are useful, that you really like or love. But how do you stay on top of things and stop clutter accumulating in your home again?

A primary cause of clutter is the 'home-less'. If you and everyone in the family dump books and papers on the kitchen table, and bags, coats, jackets on chairs, then in no time the clutter has returned. Without a home, things turn to clutter. Keeping on top of clutter starts with making sure there's a place for everything and everything in its place, so you'll need to find good homes for your stuff.

Of course, once you've decluttered you should have a lot more room – in the wardrobe, in cupboards, on shelves and in drawers – for the things you want to keep. But if you need to, change how you store things or get more appropriate (not more) storage so that you can more efficiently house your things; give all your stuff good homes.

There is more joy to be found in owning less than can ever be found in organizing more.

Joshua Becker

Don't aim to have a home that looks like a room in an interiors magazine or a John Lewis catalogue; those images are designed by a team of stylists. No one actually lives in those rooms. Instead, just aim for a place for everything. Having a place for everything makes it far less likely that things will become cluttered and untidy because everything has a home: a good space where it's easy to store things rather than stuff and jam them in or leave things lying around.

Have limited areas for clutter; areas where clutter may live freely, so long as it stays within boundaries. In your bedroom, for example, one chair – and only one chair – is the 'clothes clutter preserve'. Clothes can be thrown there but only there, on the chair.

You might have a large basket in the living room for catalogues and magazines, but both have to be regularly decluttered. Have a tray or box for incoming papers and don't put papers down anywhere but that spot. Letters to answer, forms to fill in? Put them in the inbox. Receipts and notices? In the inbox! Once the box is full, sort through it: action, file or throw out.

Stop accumulating

There are two ways to make a man richer: give him more money or curb his desires.

Jean-Jacques Rousseau

Another way to stay on top of clutter is, of course, to accumulate less; the less stuff you bring through the front door, the less clutter you will accumulate. The aim isn't to give up buying anything ever again, but to slow down the constant influx of stuff and make conscious and deliberate decisions about what you buy.

My daughter suffered from eczema as a baby. I took every single chemical out of the house – including shampoos, lotions, bleach, detergents, deodorant, wood polish – everything! I filled four large boxes just with different cleaning products. I learned I didn't need any of the products I got rid of, they were all just derivatives of oils, vinegar, baking soda, Castile soap or other old school home remedies.

Kati Berg

Buy good quality things – good quality clothes, for example – that you need, not random stuff that appeals because it's so cheap. Fashion is estimated to be one of the most polluting industries in the world. One aspect of this problem is the amount of clothes we throw out. In 2013, about 85% of America's 15.1 million tonnes of textile waste ended up in landfill. Secondhand clothes are often sent to cheap markets in the developing world, compromising local vendors' ability to compete.

Of course, an occasional purchase is a pleasure to indulge. But for many of us, we need to rein in the constant buying and accumulating.

Surf the urge to buy

'Shopper's high' is like the rush that can come with drinking or gambling. Your attention becomes fixed; you focus only on the perceived rewards, while ignoring the downside – in this case, the clutter that you'll accumulate.

Loosen the fixation; remind yourself of your good intentions. This helps to keep you focused on what matters most and can get you through the moments when your impulses try to take over.

Top Tip: Surf the urge. Any time you feel yourself tempted to buy or accept something you don't really need or love, 'surf the urge'. Imagine the urge to buy as a wave in the ocean. It will build in intensity, but soon break and dissolve. Imagine yourself riding the wave, not fighting it but also not giving in to it. Know that cravings aren't permanent, they come and then they go. Just like the waves.

Keeping your home decluttered means forming a new habit. New habits take time to establish but after the first few weeks, you may well have cracked it. Create a new habit: from now on, when you buy something new, practise the 'one in, one out' rule: for each new item that comes into your home, another one has to go. To help with this, ask yourself, 'Do I love it enough to get rid of another one I already own?'

Do the same with your children's toys. Have specific cupboards, shelves, boxes and baskets for toys. Once any cupboard, shelf, drawer, box etc. is full, there's no room to add more toys. Explain to your children that if they want to add more toys – especially at birthdays and Christmas –

they'll need to remove some too. After Christmas or birthdays, ask them to put all their gifts in one place. Then, a day or two after Christmas or their birthday, ask them to decide what they no longer want – what can be given away, or sold – so that they can make room for the new things.

Borrow, hire and rent

Learn to enjoy things without owning them. Ownership is nothing, access is everything. Visit a library, a park or a museum.

Joshua Becker

Support your local library. Borrow adult and children's fiction and non-fiction books and eBooks. DVDs, CDs, audio books, language courses, music scores and books in other languages are also available to hire. Google 'local library' and find, renew and reserve items online.

Hire, don't buy, tools for home DIY projects. Borrow garden and kitchen equipment from a friend or neighbour. Street-bank (www.streetbank.com) enables neighbours to share with each other; everything and anything from tools and instruments to cool boxes and sofa beds.

Non-clutter gifts

We don't need to increase our goods nearly as much as we need to scale down our wants.

Donald Horban

Gifts for Christmas and birthdays, weddings and anniversaries: rare is the gift-giver who wants their gift to be a burden on you or your home, but how do you accept gifts that mark these special occasions and yet remain clutter free?

Create a 'clutter-free gift list' and let family and friends know that you do have some ideas for what you'd really like that won't mean more things to store in your home. Request quality over quantity, needs over wants, experiences over products.

But just because you ask for experiences over products doesn't mean your family and friends want the same. If they would like new dancing shoes, consider buying them new dancing shoes. If they'd like another ceramic figurine to add to their collection, buy them another ceramic figurine. Giving gifts is an opportunity to show your love and appreciation; you can make your case for anti-consumerism and less clutter another time.

Be generous with your gift-giving but be generous in your gift-receiving too. Be open to receiving their gifts; accept that friends and relatives may have something they really want to give you.

Here are some ideas for clutter-free gifts to give and receive:

- Combined gifts, where several friends, colleagues or family members chip in on larger items.
- Tickets for a cinema, theatre, show, festival, music or sports event.
- iTunes or Amazon gift cards to download songs or a subscription to a music-streaming site.
- Vouchers for a restaurant, afternoon tea or spa treatment.
- Vouchers to learn a new skill: anything from flying lessons and land yachting to art, music or dance lessons.

- An experience: anything from hovercraft racing or bushcraft to flower arranging or chocolate making.
- Family gift cards or passes to a zoo, theme park or museum.
- A family photo session.
- A bus or train pass.
- Plants, flowers, cuttings and seedlings.
- Beeswax candles (they're free of additives such as paraffin).
- Services of a gardener for a day.
- Car valeting.

Finally, however careful you are not to let obvious clutter into your life, there are always going to be some things that evolve into clutter over time. You'll need to recognize when something that was once useful and valuable has evolved into clutter. Without getting obsessive about it, once or twice a year, go through each room or collection of things and ask yourself the same questions – Do I still need it? Do I still like it or love it?

In a nutshell

- Stop clutter accumulating in your home by creating new, helpful habits.
- Find good homes for your stuff; a place for everything and everything in its place.
- If necessary, change how you store things or get new, more appropriate storage so that you can more efficiently give all your things good homes.
- Have limited areas for clutter; areas where clutter may live freely, so long as it stays within boundaries.
- Accumulate less; the less stuff you bring through the front door, the less clutter you will accumulate. Make

more conscious and deliberate decisions about what you buy.

- Buy good quality things that you need, not random stuff that appeals because it's so cheap.
- Practise surfing the urge. Any time you feel yourself tempted to buy or accept something you don't really need or love, 'surf the urge'. This helps to keep you focused on what matters most and can get you through the moments when your impulses try to take over.
- Use the 'one in, one out' rule: for each new item that comes into your home, another one has to go. To help with this, ask yourself, 'Do I love it enough to get rid of another one I already own?'
- Borrow, hire and rent. Borrow books, DVDs, CDs etc. from the library. Hire tools for home DIY projects. Borrow garden and kitchen equipment from a friend or neighbour. Ask for and buy clutter-free gifts.
- Recognize when something that was once useful and valuable has evolved into clutter. Once or twice a year, go through each room or collection of things and ask yourself the same questions – Do I still need it? Do I still like it or love it?

PART 2

Declutter Your Life

What I know for sure is that when you declutter, whether it's in your home, your head, or your heart, it is astounding what will flow into that space that will enrich you, your life and your family.

Peter Walsh

6
Declutter
Your Commitments

Slow down and enjoy life. It's not only the scenery you miss by going too fast; you also miss the sense of where you're going and why.

Eddie Cantor

What's a typical week for you? What's a typical day? What do you have to do next? What haven't you done? Is there too much to do and too much to think about? Are you trying to do several things at once?

You've got too many commitments!

For so many of us, it's not that there's not enough time in the day, it's more that we're trying to do too much in the time we've got; we have too many commitments and obligations and too much to think about.

Maybe you've agreed to help out at the school fair, visit elderly relatives, babysit or show up to a friend's play, art show, band or choir performance, or cheer a colleague on as they run a marathon. Perhaps you've joined a book club, taken out a gym membership or you've taken on some voluntary work. Maybe you've joined a committee, enrolled on a course or got involved in a local, national or even global cause. On top of all that, you've got your children's play dates to organize, homework to help with, a camping trip coming up, a DIY project and you promised your Mum a day out together next weekend.

Too often, we commit to too many people and too many things, and then find ourselves without enough time to fully enjoy or complete those commitments. Just like a home that's too cluttered, if your life is already full with commitments and obligations it can be stressful.

What's the difference between commitments and obligations? A commitment is something you agree to do or choose to engage in. An obligation arises out of you choosing to commit to something. An obligation is something that you're obliged to do; you feel you *have* to out of a sense of duty because you said you would.

If you choose to commit to something, you accept the obligations. If, for example, you commit to a book club, you accept the obligation to read the chosen book each month and turn up for the meetings. If you lose interest and you no longer feel committed to the book club, those obligations become a burden.

Burdensome obligations become clutter in our lives when there's not the will to back them up. You need to choose your commitments wisely, otherwise you'll increase your obligations. And they may become burdensome obligations.

Just like too much stuff in your home can be stressful – taking up your time and energy and leaving no room for new things – too many commitments create pressure and stress and can get in the way of you doing the things you most want to do and living the life you want to live. There's also no room for newer, more interesting or enjoyable activities that are more in line with your life now.

How have you accumulated so many commitments?

Maybe you're the sort of person who over commits when you're feeling especially energetic, productive and capable. At times like this, it's easy to think you can take on and cope with more. Perhaps you're an overachiever; you feel you have to prove something to yourself or others: family, friends, colleagues and even casual acquaintances. Maybe you sign up to good causes and offer to help others out of goodwill and compassion or you feel strongly about an issue and really want to step in to help. Or perhaps you just can't say no to invitations or to other people's requests for help.

Whatever the reason for over committing yourself, as you fit more things in, you clutter your life with too many commitments and, sooner or later, it becomes too much.

Why can't you let go?

Taking a step back and disentangling yourself isn't always easy; wanting to avoid feeling guilty, wanting to keep up appearances, or fearing rejection, scorn or shame can all be reasons for why you find it difficult to let go of commitments.

It may be that you're thinking about sunk costs: the time, effort, love or money you've already put into something.

Sunk costs can fool you into sticking with something you would be best off ending, so you continue to put more time, effort or money into someone or something – the exercise classes, the political party you've been relentlessly campaigning for or Friday evening drinks with colleagues that you always go along to. Even though you're not enjoying it, you stay the course instead of letting go.

Perhaps you tell yourself you just can't; you'll let people down if you don't keep up with all your commitments. You said you would do something, so you think you should keep your word, stick with it and put up with the difficulties. But the commitment has become an obligation; you feel it's your duty. You *have* to stick with it.

It can be difficult to back out of a commitment if you're worried about the other person's response; you know the other person will be easily offended – they'll be angry or hostile in some way, ignore you or sulk – if you explain you can no longer stick with it. Maybe, for example, you promised your sister – who doesn't get out that often and loves films – that you'd go to the cinema with her once a fortnight. You've got to a point where you're resenting the commitment and you feel trapped. But you don't want to let her down and you can't face handling her reaction if you back out.

It could be that you tell yourself that you're so used to that particular commitment – you've done it for so long already – that you might as well carry on. You think they can't do it without you. Maybe you do some voluntary work – you serve tea at a hospice or do the accounts for a local community group – and you think, 'They like me. They want me. They *need* me. I can't let them down.'

Perhaps you don't want to call it a day because you don't want to admit that you were wrong to have committed to it in the first place. So you struggle on.

It doesn't have to be like this! You can declutter your commitments.

Benefits of decluttering your commitments

Just as there are benefits to decluttering your home, there are benefits to decluttering your commitments. Which of these benefits to letting go of one or more of your commitments appeals to you?

- I'll feel less stressed, pressured, burdened and put upon.
- I'll no longer waste time worrying about what I feel I 'ought' to do or I 'should' do and start focusing on the things I want to do.
- I'll have more time, energy and/or money for the commitments I choose to keep: the things I really want to do, that I enjoy and care about.

Identify your commitments

To declutter your commitments, start by identifying what they are. Make a list. Look at everything you've got going on in a typical day, week and month: going to work, routines and commitments at home, family members' needs and activities, your own hobbies, interests and projects. Write them down. Which of the things on your list do you recognize as things you absolutely have to do – go to work, care for someone else – children or a vulnerable family member, for example? These are the activities, tasks and duties that are probably non-negotiable – you need or have to keep them.

Identify your values

Next, think about your values – what's important to you and has some worth. Here are some examples:

- Time with family.
- Time with friends.
- Your physical health.
- Your mental health.
- Time for your current interests and hobbies.
- Time to learn new skills and knowledge.
- Time to do absolutely nothing. To be quiet, calm and relax.

What relationships, work, activities etc. are most important to you? Think about which of these you enjoy doing. Which of these are in line with your values? What's important to you? For each commitment, ask yourself, 'How much does it matter to me? Is it something that's important to me; in line with my values and priorities?'

Identify what to let go of

Identify how you feel about each commitment. Write down each commitment and then write down how you feel about each one. Feelings of stress, anxiety, irritation and resentment for any one commitment are telling you to let go. Maybe it's something you used to enjoy but you no longer like doing; it even annoys you, the thought of doing it makes you feel stressed.

Perhaps a particular commitment is no longer relevant or appropriate in your life – being a primary school governor, for example, has no interest for you since both your children have now moved on to secondary school.

Apply the keep/don't keep principle to your commitments. Think about what you really need to keep. What can you let go of, not do or not go to? What can you give away, delegate and get someone else to do? If it doesn't feel good, let it go knowing that what's left is more in line with what you need and want to do with your time.

Move on

Now think about what you would like to make more room for in your life.

Maybe you want more time for reading or watching films, more time with your partner, children or other family or friends. Perhaps you'd like time to explore new activities – drop the community work to take up singing in a choir or rock climbing, for example. Maybe you simply want to do less of anything.

Top Tip: Set limits. Decide how many commitments and obligations are enough in any one day, week or month. Instead of trying to cram too much into every day, move at a slower, more relaxed pace and get the most out of what you're doing now. Leave room between activities and tasks. Take time to do what you're doing instead of looking for ways that you can fit more in. If you fill your days with things to do, you will always be trying to get ahead of yourself.

Ditch the guilt

If you can change your mind, you can change your life.

William James

If you find it difficult to admit that you made a mistake, realize that, at the time you committed yourself, you made the right choice. So, yes, you agreed to be on the committee or you signed up to a 12-week Pilates class. Now, however, you realize you made a decision too quickly; what you thought you wanted to do doesn't now seem such a good idea after all.

Perhaps your circumstances have changed and you have new options. It could be that what you've now decided you do or don't want to do is more in line with your abilities, is more realistic and achievable for you. Maybe you've simply had a change of heart; your feelings about a situation have changed.

Top Tip: Think positive. See yourself as open-minded, flexible and able to change and adapt according to new circumstances. See yourself as simply having made a new decision.

You can always draw something good out. At the very least, you'll have learnt something about yourself. For example, you now know that exercise classes are not for you; that to maintain your fitness levels you're better off doing a lot more walking or something else you enjoy.

Whatever commitments you're holding onto, ask yourself why. Is it because you need or want to keep the commitment or because you want to avoid feeling guilty or rejected by others?

Use your courage! You may well feel concerned, worried or anxious about telling someone else that you're going to stop doing whatever it is you had previously committed to. That's OK. But rather than focus on how anxious you feel, think of how much better you'll feel for having done so. Having a few uncomfortable conversations is a small price to pay for freeing yourself from commitments that you have begun to resent and that are making you unhappy.

James, for example, realized that if he wanted to further his career in marketing, he would need to get some qualifications. With encouragement from his manager, he enrolled on a Diploma in Marketing course.

After the first module – which was three months long – James was struggling. 'Attending the class once a week was not a problem,' explains James. 'But there was a lot of homework each week. Trying to combine the studying and a full-time job wasn't easy but I persevered. I told myself I should keep going. Half way through the second module I was totally stressed out and I had little time for my friends or family. Eventually I quit. What I had already learnt on the course had enabled me to get a new role at work anyway, so I decided I didn't need the qualification. I certainly didn't need the stress, it was making me miserable.

'Rather than feel bad about quitting, I saw it as "letting go" and I focused instead on what I'd gained. I applied the knowledge I had already gained from the course to my new job. And I got my life back! Less stress and more time with friends and family.'

Perhaps you don't want to lose the time, energy or money you've already invested? Like James, think about what you have to gain rather than what you have to lose by pulling out. Whether you've put up with it for a month, a year or even half a lifetime, you shouldn't carry on letting yourself be miserable just because you think all that past misery would be wasted otherwise. The past is in the past. Don't let the past dictate the present. What matters is how you live your life now; what commitments you choose to keep.

Unless you signed a contract, there's nothing to stop you from walking away. You may feel uncomfortable – you've got to explain your change of mind to friends, family or colleagues – but remember, having a few uncomfortable conversations is a small price to pay for what's right for you from now on.

If your commitment was to someone else, let them down gently and suggest an alternative way forward for them. For example, after telling your sister you're pulling out of regularly going to the cinema together, you might say, 'I'm sorry and I know you're disappointed, why don't you come round to me sometimes and we can watch a film at home?' Or, 'How about asking your neighbour? You mentioned she likes going to the cinema now and again.'

Other people might need someone filling your role but it doesn't have to be you. If you left the situation tomorrow – left the committee, for example – in three months' time what do you think would happen to those people who 'need' you? They'll adjust and, quite soon, they will be fine. People can and will sort it out. But if you stay in the situation in which you feel trapped, in three months' time will you be fine?

Say no

Learn to say no. This is a key skill to help declutter your time and simplify your life. If you can't say no to other people you'll find yourself taking on too much.

There are a number of steps involved in turning down other people's requests and demands for your time.

Notice how you feel

Firstly, when someone asks you to commit to something – helping out, attending a meeting, taking on a new project – notice how you feel; be aware of the physical feelings. Maybe your stomach flips, you feel tension in your jaw, your heartbeat increases. Perhaps your breathing becomes more rapid and shallow and your head feels like it's tightening up. That's your body telling you that you don't want to do it!

Ask for more time or information

If, though, you're not sure whether you want to commit to something, ask for more information so that you're clear what's involved. Don't be afraid to ask for time to think about it before you commit yourself. If the other person says they need an answer immediately (they have a right to do this) then rather than saying yes and regretting it later, it's best if you say no now.

Be honest, clear and succinct

When you recognize that you don't want to do something – whether it's to be a school governor, sign up for a fun run, accompany a friend to the pub quiz, see a band or watch a Shakespeare play in the park – be clear, direct and succinct. Simply say, 'Thanks for asking, but I'm not going to be able to do that'. Or, 'Thanks for asking, but the pub quiz/the band/ Shakespeare is not my thing.' Avoid waffling, rambling or giving excuses. Don't blame someone or something else, just be honest.

Give just one reason
You only need one genuine reason for saying no. Just say what you need to say.

Say, for example, 'I'm sorry, I'm not going to be able to continue to run the weekly parent and toddler group/go with you for a bike ride every Sunday morning. I need the time to visit my Mum.' Rather than, 'I'm sorry, I would do it but I've got so much on recently; I'm up to my eyes in it and I can hardly think straight sometimes and now my Mum is asking me to visit more often since her accident. I hope you don't mind too much. Sorry.'

Acknowledge what the other person thinks and says but stand your ground
Once you've said what you've got to say, say no more. Just listen to the other person's response. Then acknowledge their response but stand your ground.

For example, if you were standing down from voluntarily running the parent and toddler group: 'I understand you need someone to run the group (acknowledging their response) but after next month it will have to be someone else (standing your ground).'

Or, in another example, if you were turning down a social invitation: 'I know you were hoping I'd come with you (acknowledging their response) but I really don't like histor- ical re-enactments (standing your ground). Thanks for asking though.'

Whether you say no to people face to face, with a phone call or by email, just be honest with people and tell them that you're not going to commit; you're going to say no.

Stand your ground or negotiate and compromise

If you want to, do stand your ground. But you may also decide to negotiate or compromise with the other person.

For example, you might say, 'I could ask any of the other parents if they'd be prepared to run the group' or 'You could ask Emma or Mo to come with you to the historical re-enactment. I expect they'd be pleased to be asked.'

New commitments

Be careful about saying yes to new commitments; be aware of requests for your time as potential obligations. If you think you're going to agree to do something, ask yourself why you're agreeing to it. Is it something that you'll enjoy doing? Ask yourself what is in it for you. You don't always have to benefit, but it will help you narrow things down.

Top Tip: Take the 'one in, one out' approach; for every new commitment you agree to, think which activity you're currently committed to that you could drop.

You can still be perfectly nice and sociable but aim to be more of your true self; aim to focus more on people and things that you care about and are important to you. There's no point feigning enthusiasm for an event – a party, for example – only to spend the next couple of weeks resenting the obligation to attend. Reserve your time, energy and money for things that are important to you, that you need to do or that you enjoy or care about.

Those things might change in future; be flexible and be prepared to review your commitments now and again. Are you still enjoying them? Are they important and do you care about them?

In a nutshell

- Too many commitments create pressure and stress and can get in the way of doing the things you most want to do. There's also no room for newer, more interesting or enjoyable activities that are more in line with your life now.
- There are a number of reasons why you might over commit; perhaps you think you can take on and cope with more. Maybe you're an overachiever: you feel you have to prove something to yourself or others. It could be that you commit to help others out of goodwill or you feel strongly about an issue and really want to do something about it. Or perhaps you just can't say no to invites or to other people's requests for help.
- Sunk costs, not wanting to let other people down, avoiding guilt, wanting to keep up appearances, fear of rejection, scorn or shame can all be reasons why you find it difficult to let go of commitments.
- There are benefits to decluttering your commitments: you'll feel less stressed and less put upon. You won't waste time worrying about what you feel you 'ought' to do or you 'should' do. You'll have more time, energy and/or money for the things you really need and want to do, that you enjoy.

- Identify your commitments. For each commitment, ask yourself, 'How much does it matter to me? Is it something that's important to me, in line with my values and priorities?'
- Identify what to let go of. Feelings of stress, anxiety, irritation and resentment for any one commitment are telling you to let go.
- Apply the keep/don't keep principle to your commitments. Think about what you really need to keep. What can you let go of, not do or not go to? What can you give away, delegate and get someone else to do?
- Ditch the guilt. Realize that, at the time you committed yourself, you made the right choice. Don't let the past dictate the present. What matters is how you live your life now; what commitments you choose to keep.
- Think about what you have to gain rather than what you have to lose by pulling out.
- Unless you signed a contract, there's nothing to stop you from walking away. You may feel uncomfortable – you've got to explain your change of mind to friends, family or colleagues – but it's a small price to pay for what's right for you from now on.
- If your commitment was to someone else, let them down gently and suggest an alternative way forward for them.
- Other people might need someone filling your role but it doesn't have to be you. If you leave the situation, they'll adjust and they will sort it out. But if you stay in that situation, will *you* be fine?
- Be careful about saying yes to new commitments. Take the 'one in, one out' approach: for every new commitment you agree to, think which activity you're currently committed to that you could drop.

- Learn to say no. This is a key skill to help declutter your time and simplify your life. If you can't say no to other people, you'll find yourself taking on too much.
- Set limits. Decide how many commitments and obligations are enough in any one day, week or month. Instead of trying to cram too much into every day, leave room between commitments. Take time to do what you're doing instead of looking for ways that you can fit more in.
- Review your commitments now and again. Are you still enjoying them? Are they important and do you care about them?

7
Declutter Your Friendships

We have three types of friends in life: friends for a reason,
friends for a season and friends for a lifetime.

Author unknown

How many friends and acquaintances do you have? What type of friends are they? More than two thousand years ago, the Greek philosopher Aristotle identified three different kinds of friendship: friendships of utility, friendships of pleasure and friendships of virtue.

Friendships of utility are friendships of mutual benefit: one way or another, the relationship is useful to both you and the other person. That person could be a colleague, customer or client or, for example, a neighbour with whom you exchange each other's gardening or household tools, feed the cat and check each other's houses when you go on holiday.

Friendships of pleasure exist between you and those with whom you enjoy a shared interest: people in the same sports team as you, a book club, choir, dance class etc. It could be the people you met on holiday; you had a great time together (and insisted you'd keep in touch.)

But both types of friendships usually end when circumstances change; when a friendship of utility is no longer beneficial to one or both of you, one of you leaves the job or the neighbour moves away. Friendships of pleasure also often end when what you have in common comes to an end: when one or both of you leave the team, the club, the class or the holiday comes to an end.

Friendships of virtue are based on mutual respect and admiration. These friendships may take more time to establish than the other two kinds, but they're also stronger and more enduring. They often arise when two people recognize that they have similar values and goals; that they have similar visions for how their lives and the world should be. Often, they begin when a person is young – at school, college or holiday jobs – though plenty form after that, too.

Aristotle pointed out that there can't be a large number of friends in a virtuous friendship group because the amount of time and care that this type of friendship needs limits the amount of time you can spend with other friends.

Fast forward to the 21st century and not much has changed. Anthropologist and evolutionary biologist Professor Robin Dunbar agrees that there's a limit to the number of friendships that any one person can have. He suggests we maintain a series of social networks. One hundred and fifty is the number of people we know as casual friends – those met through work or a leisure interest or the people you'd invite to a big party but with whom your relationship never turns into anything deeper. Most relationships in this group have a natural life cycle. Often, we're drawn together by circumstance – work, the single life, children – and, as Aristotle noted, as our situations change, we tend to go our separate ways.

The next group of people – 50 – is the number of people you would know as friends. You see them often, but not so much that you consider them to be true intimates. Then there's the circle of 15: the good friends that you can turn to for a degree of support when you need it. The most intimate in 'Dunbar's number' – five – is your close support group. These are your best friends and may include family members.

People move in and out of these different friendship groups and sometimes fall out of them altogether. Too often, though, we accumulate and hold onto friendships that no longer serve a purpose or have any pleasure in them. Despite what the Spice Girls sang, it's not true that friendship never ends. So why do we hold on?

Why we hold on

Maybe you have a friendship where you're becoming more and more unhappy. Despite the problems, you refuse to recognize that it's time to let the friendship die and, instead, push on in the hope that things will get better between you.

Do you, for example, tough it out with a friend who is struggling with addiction? Can you stay friends with someone when you realize that you have major differences of opinion about a world situation – it dawns on you that their political values, for example, are fundamentally different from yours?

Or do you tell yourself that you don't want to be a fair-weather friend; that friendship isn't just about having fun?

Of course, over time the balance will shift back and forth; you will inevitably have a problem or difficulty at the same time your friend has some wonderful things going on in their life. But while friendships often have ups and downs, if the downs are too extreme or too frequent, what do you do? Friends are supposed to add to your life, not take away from it.

Friendships are often driven by what we think of as duty; there's a sense of loyalty and we feel obliged to be friends with some people. We feel guilty – that we're doing something wrong – if we let go. But if you're not spending a lot of time together and don't have much in common any more, it really is OK to let that friendship go. The fact they are no longer a colleague or your neighbour doesn't mean you have to meet for dinner every six months. Sending a Christmas card is enough.

On the other hand, perhaps it's not that you're worried you'll regret letting go, it's more that you're hoping you will spend more time with a particular friend. You tell yourself, 'When I have more time, energy or money or when my kids grow up, I will get round to seeing them more often.'

Really? Will you? Are you sure about that? Be honest with yourself. Thinking like this about friends you no longer get round to seeing just serves to remind you...well, it just serves to remind you of what you still haven't got round to: meeting up with those friends.

It could be that you can't let go because you feel you've put so much into the friendship in the past that it'd be a waste of all those years to let go now. But whether you were friends for a month, a year or even half a lifetime, just as you can acknowledge that things in your home – certain books, clothes etc. – were part of your life at some point in the past, they're not now. That time has gone. Trying to keep old friendships alive – holding onto a friendship that can't be brought back – just ties you to the past. Live in the present!

However, it may be that you find it difficult to call it quits on a friendship that's no longer working for you because you just don't know how to do it kindly and gracefully. Unfriending someone you used to know on Facebook at the press of a button is not the same thing as navigating your way out of a friendship face to face.

Who to keep

Before you think about who to let go of, think about who to keep – who do you like, love and need in your life right now? Which friendships are the friendships of pleasure? These will be the friends whose company you currently enjoy as part of a shared interest – a hobby or a sport, community or voluntary work.

Other friendships to keep are those from which you both derive a mutual benefit; the friendship is useful to both of you in some way. It may be a friendship with your colleague, customer, client or neighbour.

Of course, you most definitely want to keep the 'friendships of virtue': the small number – maybe one or two, but it could be five or six – of close friends with whom you share a mutual respect and admiration, have similar values and goals, and have similar visions for how your lives and the world should be. These are people with whom you feel you can be yourself; you feel good when you're with them, you can talk to them if you're worried and they encourage you and value you.

Relationships that allow you to have fun, be happy and contribute beyond yourself; these are the friendships to look after and keep.

Who to let go

Champagne for my real friends, real pain for my sham friends.

Francis Bacon

There are three types of friendships to let go of:

- Friendships where you no longer have much in common.
- Friendships that are draining.
- Friendships that are toxic.

The friendships where you no longer have much in common are the ones where, because of a change in circumstances, the relationship is no longer beneficial to both of you. This could be, for example, a colleague, client or neighbour; one of you leaves the job, or the neighbour moves away. Other friendships to let go of are the friendships of pleasure – when what you have in common comes to an end; when one or both of you leave the team, the club, the class etc. You quite literally go your separate ways. It's perfectly normal; you no longer have anything to keep you connected.

These relationships, although they were sincere and genuine, came out of convenience. But once the circumstances have changed, if maintaining the friendship is too much like hard work, it's time to let go and move on.

You can declutter old colleagues, school friends, university friends, neighbours, not with any malice but simply because you don't have the time to see them. Or the inclination. If you feel you 'ought' to rather than you just want to, it's probably not going to last in a strong, connected way in any case.

The second type of friendship to let go of are friendships that are draining. Keeping these friendships alive can feel like pushing a piano up a hill; it's too much like hard work.

Some friendships simply run their course. Maybe you realize you want different things; you no longer share the same interests. You've grown apart. The friend, for example, who won't see you without bringing her dull partner or wild children along – or both. Ask yourself whether you can do without the relationship or whether it's something you unquestionably still want.

You're bound to outgrow certain friendships. Once you're aware of that, without being cruel or feeling guilt-ridden, you can begin to let go of friendships you no longer need or enjoy; that you realize no longer fit.

What about the third type of friendship to let go of – the toxic friend? Who is this person? Toxic friends are the friends – the no-gooders – whose 'friendship' is making you unhappy or miserable. Sometimes it's obvious: a so-called friend steals your money or your partner. Or they're blatantly using you – an ex-sister-in-law who is only being friends as a way of finding out what your brother – her ex-husband – is up to.

Other times it's not so obvious. We've all had friends who have gone through difficulties – addiction, relationship break-up, bereavement, financial problems. When this happens it doesn't mean that you should walk away. But if, over the months and years, you do all the emotional work – talking them down, shoring them up – 'Of course you're not to blame for what's happened in your life. Sure, let's talk about your problems. Again.' – and they're never around if you need them, it's time to pull the plug.

The righteous choose their friends carefully, but the way of the wicked leads them astray.

Proverbs 12.26

A toxic friend is someone who does one or more of the following:

- Is not pleased for you when something good has happened in your life.
- Mostly talks about themselves and rarely asks about, let alone shows interest in, you and your life.
- Is only ever generous in your friendship if they are in pole position.
- Allows you to initiate all the ideas, make all the plans and be responsible for changing them if they're not convenient for them.
- Is over sensitive – your friendship is like walking on eggshells.
- Puts you down or winds you up.
- Competes with you.
- Embarrasses you in front of others.
- Can make you doubt yourself, your opinions, ideas and abilities.
- Belittles you – makes snide comments about your job, your cooking, what you wear or how you look.

- Doesn't encourage you or believe in you.
- Has betrayed your trust.
- Isn't loyal, doesn't stand up for you.
- Tries to sell you something, or often asks to borrow money.
- Keeps tabs on favours – for example, 'You owe me babysitting because I took care of your dog'.
- Reveals racist, sexist or political views that are totally at odds with yours.
- Is critical of others – constantly bitching about your mutual friends.
- Leaves you feeling irritated and depressed because of their negativity.

We've all held onto someone whose friendship is really hard work. Sure, you may have shared many of life's essentials – the same class and childhood friends, holidays, hairdressers, phobias and health scares, concerns about relationships, parents and your children – but if you have a toxic friend it's time to get rid of them. If every time you agree to meet or chat you dread the idea of calling or seeing that person, remove them from your life!

Breaking up is not easy. Indeed, there must have been a time when you were good friends; you liked each other. But you're not a bad person because you no longer like someone. Far better, surely, to remember the good times, cut loose and move forward.

Benefits of letting go

Maintaining friendships that no longer work is like having things in your home that need constant attention and repair. Instead of acquiring friends and holding onto them, letting go of some friendships ensures the people in your life are there because you value them and not just because you were friends in the past, you feel guilty etc. Like clearing clothes from a wardrobe, which leaves space for new things, letting go of friends who no longer fit leaves time, energy and resources for good friends and new friends.

Here's Natalia's experience:

A year ago we moved seventy miles away. I decluttered the house but I tried to keep hold of some of my old friends – they weren't really good friends, but friends anyway. Mostly friends I'd made through the children – parents of their friends. I recently let go of some of them. Now, I've got room – time and energy – for the mums in the town I moved to. I can say yes to local things at the weekend because I'm no longer jumping in the car and driving across three counties to visit the neighbours and the mums I used to know from the kids' school.

The women I've recently completed a women's social media training course with; we regularly text and email and meet up every couple of weeks. We support each other professionally and personally, offering advice on everything from the best apps and blogs for freelancers to how to manage toddler tantrums. I still have my four really good friends: the women I've known since I was 12. Even though two of them live miles away, if I'm going to travel anywhere at weekends, they're the people I'm happy to do it for.

How to end a friendship

So, while some friendships last throughout life, some make us feel like we've been sentenced to life. How do you cut yourself free?

Whether it's because you realize you can't stand seeing someone ever again, you no longer have anything in common or you simply don't have the time for that friendship, unless you want a full-on confrontation, aim to do it gracefully with as little distress and as few hurt feelings as possible.

Option 1: Let it fade out

There's a difference between ending a friendship and letting it fade; if the friend has harmed you in some way – betrayed or hurt you in a way that can't be ignored or forgiven – then you may want to confront them or just cut them off immediately. But if the friendship has simply run its course, then let it fade. Rather than abruptly stop calling, texting or emailing, slowly let contact diminish.

Try not returning every phone call and not initiating plans to meet up. Take your time to return texts and emails or don't return them at all. Claim to be very busy or have other excuses not to accept invitations to get together.

Saying you have a busy summer and can't fix a date, for example, will help distance you from the people you no longer want to spend time with. Try and keep your excuses as honest as possible – don't say your Mum is ill and you have to spend a lot of time with her if that's not true. But if you do have a lot going on with family members, your children, work or travel and holidays etc., then use that as a more honest reason.

Although fading out a friendship in this way – with what can be called 'passive rejection' – avoids direct confrontation and minimizes hurt feelings, it can take a while and requires an element of dishonesty which can feel uncomfortable. The alternative, however, is harder and harsher; 'Look, Ali, I just don't want to be your friend. I have neither the time or the energy so I'm letting you go.'

Option 2: Cut the friendship short

If, though, you've decided that you want to break up with your friend and let them know why, don't be unkind about it. Don't dump three years' worth of resentment on their lap. If you want to explain, do it in a way that's informative rather than judgmental and overly critical. Decide in advance what you're going to say. See if you can say it in just two or three sentences. Be prepared for them to react with comments about you. Simply acknowledge what they've said, then repeat what you've said and move on. For example: 'Okay, I understand that you think I've let you down and not been there for you. But I just can't listen to you talk endlessly in detail each time you get sacked or walk out of a job. Our friendship feels one sided – you never seem to be interested in me and what's going on in my life.'

Once you've made the break, let it go. Really let it go.

Whether you choose to let a friendship fade out or you cut it short, you might miss them now and again or look back with fond memories but you'll find that the main feeling each time is one of relief. And, on the other side, the path is clear for you to meet new people or to spend more time with the people or the things that really matter in your life.

In a nutshell

- Greek philosopher Aristotle identified three different kinds of friendship: friendships of utility, friendships of pleasure and friendships of virtue.

- People move in and out of these different friendship groups and sometimes fall out of them altogether. Too often, though, we hang onto friendships that no longer serve a purpose or have any pleasure in them.
- Maybe you can't let go because you've put so much into the friendship in the past that you feel it would be a waste of all those years to let go now. Perhaps you feel obliged to keep a friendship going – you'd feel guilty if you tried to let go. You might even regret it.
- Trying to keep old friendships alive – holding onto a friendship that can't be brought back – just ties you to the past. Live in the present!
- Maintaining friendships that no longer work is like having things in your home that need constant attention and repair.
- If you're not spending a lot of time together or don't have much in common any more, it really is OK to let that friendship go.
- Before you think about who to let go of, think about who to keep – who do you like, love and need in your life right now? Which friendships are currently the friendships of pleasure and the friendships of utility?
- There are three types of friendship to let go of:
  - Friendships where you no longer have much in common.
  - Friendships that are draining.
  - Friendships that are toxic.
- Like clearing clothes from a wardrobe, which leaves space for new things, letting go of friends who no longer fit leaves time, energy and resources for good friends and new friends.
- Unless you want a full-on confrontation, aim to do it gracefully with as little distress and as few hurt feelings

as possible. Rather than abruptly stop calling, texting or emailing, slowly let contact diminish.

- If, though, you've decided that you want to break up with your friend and let them know why, be prepared for them to react with comments about you. Simply acknowledge what they've said, repeat what you've said and move on.
- Whether you choose to let a friendship fade out or you cut it short, you might miss them now and again or look back with fond memories, but you'll find that the main feeling each time is one of relief.

8
Declutter Your Work

Is your work day made up of an endless list of things to be done? There's too much to do and too much to think about. It's difficult to think clearly; your mind is cluttered with what you're doing, what you haven't done and what you've yet to do.

There are ways you can simplify your working day!

The 80:20 principle – the 'law of the vital few' that suggests that we wear 20% of our clothes or use 20% of our things 80% of the time – applies to your workload too. Aim to identify and engage yourself with the important or urgent 20% of your workload and clear out the other 80%.

Yes, you need to prioritize and plan. But decluttering your day is also about knowing how to optimize your time, manage interruptions and distractions, and delegate.

First, write down everything you can think of that needs to be done on any one day or that week. Don't keep it on different post-it notes or in your head. There are benefits to making a list.

Making a list:

- Empties your head – once you've written down all the things you have to do, all your 'to do's are no longer cluttering up your mind.
- Reassures you that you haven't overlooked or forgotten anything.
- Gives you an overview of what does and doesn't need to be done.
- Helps you to prioritize and plan what you do and don't need to do.
- Helps you feel more in control.

No doubt you've been told before that working from a 'to do' list is the way to get more organized and simplify your day, but often, once you've written everything down, just looking at all the things on the list can leave you feeling stressed and overwhelmed. The answer is to create *separate* lists. Just as putting all your things into separate drawers and shelves helps to organize things in your home, so having separate lists can help you more clearly see the different kinds of tasks you have ahead of you. So, have separate lists and don't have more than six or seven tasks on each one.

If you were a freelance journalist, your lists might include:

- Stories to research.
- Editors to pitch new ideas to.
- Potential interviewees for the article I'm currently writing.
- Invoices to send.

But, more generally, whatever your job, those separate lists could be:

- Important and urgent.
- Not urgent but important.

- Not important but urgent.
- Not important or urgent.

What's important? What's urgent?

At the beginning of each day or week, decide what you actually need to get done and want to get done. What are you aiming to achieve?

Whichever tasks you choose to work on in any one day, plan the tasks. Planning is different from worrying. Worrying about everything you need to do slows you down because worrying clutters and overwhelms your brain. In contrast, planning involves clearly identifying what you need to do and thinking through how you will do it: the steps you'll need to take. It's easier to get straight on to the next step if you have already planned what and how you are going to do something.

Whatever task or job you begin your day with, decide what's the first thing you're going to do towards that task. Then do that one thing. Be mindful; give it your full attention. Once that one thing is done, do the next step. Give that your full attention too. Be deliberate and purposeful, not rushed and random.

Rethink multi-tasking

Don't try and multi-task. Single task instead. Multi-tasking is not doing several things at once. Trying to do more than one thing at a time – finding some information while talking on the phone or writing an email while thinking about the next three things you've got to do – clutters up your time and your mind. Your concentration isn't completely focused on any of the tasks; your brain is trying to cope with too many things at one time.

To multi-task successfully you do one thing at a time and you focus on it completely. Then you move onto the next task or activity.

So, at any one point in the day, be clear about what you are going to work on. Then, decide how much time to give each task your full focus. Do it deliberately and completely. Then move on to the thing you need or want to do. Approaching your workload this way is taking a mindful approach; you simply focus on what you are doing right now, at the present time, instead of cluttering your mind with what else you've got to do.

In what's known in psychology as the 'Zeigarnik effect', uncompleted tasks typically keep popping back up into your mind. If, however, you've made a list, whenever thoughts about other work pop into your mind, you can remind yourself that you won't forget them because they're on your list. If you do start thinking about what else you have to do, pause, acknowledge that those thoughts have come into your mind, and then pull yourself back to refocus on what you're doing right now.

Optimize your time

To help you further plan and simplify your workload, it can help to know your optimal times of the day: the times in the day when your physical and mental energy and concentration levels are at their best.

Some tasks, such as researching, reading or writing bids and reports, need all your focus and concentration. However, it's not a good use of time and energy if you try to do these things at a time of day that doesn't work for you. It's difficult to be focused and engaged and you're more likely to be easily distracted. On the other hand, getting things done at your optimal time of day will take less effort and energy because it's easier for you to focus and concentrate on what's happening and what needs doing.

Think whether you're a morning, afternoon or evening person. If you're not sure, try out different times of day and different amounts of time on various activities to see when you have the most mental and physical energy. Identify what sort of jobs or activities you can only spend a short time on. Are you easily bored or distracted by some tasks? Probably best to do them when your ability to focus is at its highest: at your optimal time of day.

Of course, your job may not allow you to choose when you do particular tasks or activities so you'll have to be flexible and work out the best compromise possible. However, even if you plan, prioritize and optimize your time, it's not easy to keep focused and engaged when distractions, interruptions and meetings clutter up your time.

Managing interruptions

Interruptions can arrive unexpectedly at any time of day. They come from other people in the form of questions, announcements, requests and demands, by people who need decisions made, conflicts managed and problems solved. Interruptions come in person or by phone, text or email.

Interruptions may feel like they are not within your control, but they can be managed.

To start with, accept that interruptions will happen. Then plan for them. This means leaving gaps in your day for interruptions; allow 25% of your time for interruptions and other delays.

Other people will interrupt you only if they know that you will respond. Set times that you are available to deal with their problems and questions. Then you can deal with problems and requests at certain times of the day, and focus on your work during other times. If someone interrupts you with a query and you think it needs discussion, tell the person that you will you get back to them at a later time that day when you're free to give it your full attention.

Set criteria for other people interrupting you, so that only decisions above a certain level of importance will come to you. Delegate; if you're in a supervisory or management position, where all queries and decisions must come through you, it's inevitable that you're going to be interrupted, so train others to make these decisions. Set guidelines for making decisions so that they'd make pretty much the same decision as you in any given situation.

If you can't avoid interruptions, then deal with interruptions one at a time. Give your full attention to each person and each query or problem. This way, you will be less stressed and more able to deal calmly and fully with every person who needs your attention.

Be assertive. Learn to say 'no' to requests or tasks if you are busy, if it is not an important task, if someone else can handle it or if it can be done later. Saying no to unimportant things – too many emails, meetings and taking on unnecessary projects – means that you can say yes to important things, the things you want to do, that need doing and that you like doing.

Avoiding distractions

Interruptions divert your attention and break into your time – and usually come from other people. A distraction also diverts your attention, but it's something that you *allow* yourself to be diverted by. Whether it's emails, text messages, social media, surfing the internet or someone stopping by your desk for a chat, distractions clutter up your time and take you away from what you are meant to be doing.

A distraction is not a distraction unless you pay attention to it. Anticipate your needs before you do something that needs your full attention – whether you'll need particular information, resources or just something to drink, get what you need and you'll be less likely to be drawn away from what you intended to focus on. Only you know what the distractions are and only you can avoid, manage or minimize them. If it's your phone or emails that distract you, turn them off. If you get 20 emails and texts a day, this means 20 distractions to your day. Stop reading every email as it arrives. Switch off instant alerts and, instead, choose a specific time when you will check your inbox. Go somewhere where you're not distracted by other people or put headphones on and listen to music to stay focused.

If you feel tempted by a distraction, tell yourself that you will get to it in your break, but not sooner. Any time you realize you've allowed yourself to be distracted, don't berate yourself, just return to what you were doing. Tell yourself, 'I know I lost focus, but now I'm going to continue with what I'm doing.'

Cut down on meetings

Do you sometimes feel like you spend more time sitting in meetings than actually working? Too many teams get into the habit of weekly meetings, even if there's nothing new to discuss. The answer? Leave a meeting or don't go to it in the first place. It may be a bold move, but if you've nothing to contribute and nothing to gain, why let it clutter up your time?

Aim not to avoid all meetings, but to keep the useful ones and cut out the meetings that aren't. How do you identify the least productive meetings, the ones to let go of? Ask yourself the following questions:

Is there a clear agenda or a framework to structure the meeting? If you're invited to a meeting that doesn't have an agenda, ask the organizer if they could provide one so that you can decide if it's going to cover anything that's important and relevant to you and your work.

Is the agenda actionable? A productive meeting has an actionable agenda, which defines the desired outcomes of the meeting. If it doesn't have an actionable agenda but you can't skip the meeting, steer it in the right direction by suggesting you all identify actions that will follow as a result of the meeting.

Is the meeting veering off subject? Getting off the subject is probably the number one challenge to meeting productivity: agenda items are left untouched. If someone goes off at a tangent that is only marginally related to the designated topic and the person chairing the meeting doesn't intervene, you might have to. Simply say, 'I'm concerned we're not going to have enough time for this – could we get back to the main subject?'

Can I leave early?   Don't be afraid to cut it short; if the meeting is dragging on and there's nothing on the agenda that you need to be there for, let it go. Excuse yourself and leave.

Would a short, one-to-one conversation be better?   Is there an hour's meeting scheduled to discuss something that would take a 10-minute discussion or an email to sort out? If so, walk over to the person and talk to them or send the email.

Is your entire team going to a meeting that doesn't directly impact the team?   If so, suggest one of you attends – a team representative – who can brief everyone else later.

It *is* possible to say no to a meeting. Think carefully about which meetings to keep to – which ones are absolutely necessary – and which you can let go of.

Give it away: delegate

Review your workload regularly. Is there one task that always ends up at the bottom of the pile? If you find you're avoiding it, can somebody else do it? Consider delegating whole projects that you don't need to be involved in.

Why clutter up your day spending your time doing tasks that others may have the time and ability to do? Delegating work will give you more time to focus on what's most important, useful, necessary or even enjoyable! When you delegate, not only are you free to focus on what you – and maybe only you – can do well, but you also free yourself to take on new opportunities and challenges and gain new experience.

Just as letting go of things in your home and giving them away benefits other people, delegating tasks and activities to others also benefits others. They gain new skills and abilities. Even if you have to train them – show them how to do something first – you're giving them more responsibility and authority. This could have the added benefit of new ideas and solutions to problems emerging that you may not have identified!

Top Tip: Over the next couple of weeks, write down all the tasks and activities your job involves and then categorize them according to your level of skill and enjoyment. The key to success is to focus as much of your time as possible on using your skills and strengths and delegate everything else.

In a nutshell

- There *are* ways you can simplify your working day! Aim to identify and engage yourself with the important or urgent 20% of your workload and clear out the other 80%.
- You need to prioritize and plan. But decluttering your day is also about knowing how to optimize your time, manage interruptions and distractions and delegate.
- Writing a list is a way to get more organized but often, once you've written everything down, just looking at

all the things on the list can leave you feeling stressed and overwhelmed.

- Create *separate* lists. Just as putting all your things into separate drawers and shelves helps to organize things in your home, so having separate lists – with six or seven tasks on each one – can help you more clearly see the different kinds of tasks you have ahead of you.
- At the beginning of each day or week, decide what you actually need to get done and want to get done. What's important? What's urgent? What are you aiming to achieve?
- Multi-tasking is not doing several things at once. Trying to do more than one thing at a time clutters up your time and your mind. To multi-task successfully, you do one thing at a time and you focus on it completely. Then you move onto the next task or activity. Give that your full attention too.
- It can help to know your optimal times of the day: the times in the day when your physical and mental energy and concentration levels are at their best.
- Accept that interruptions will happen. Then plan for them. Leave gaps in your day for interruptions: allow 25% of your time for interruptions and other delays.
- Set times when you are available to deal with other people's problems and questions. Set criteria for other people interrupting you. Delegate: train others to make decisions.
- A distraction is not a distraction unless you pay attention to it. Anticipate your needs and remove potential distractions before you do something that needs your full attention.
- Aim to keep the useful meetings and cut out the meetings that aren't. Ask yourself: Is there a clear, actionable agenda? Is the meeting veering off subject? Can I leave

early? Would a short, one-to-one conversation be better? Could just one of my team attend and report back to the rest of us?

- Delegating work will give you more time to focus on what's most important, useful, necessary and enjoyable. You'll also free yourself to take on new opportunities and challenges and gain new experience.
- Just as letting go of things in your home and giving them away benefits other people, delegating tasks and activities to others also benefits others. They gain new skills and abilities.
- Learn to say 'no' to requests or tasks if you are busy, if it is not an important task, if someone else can handle it or if it can be done later. Saying no to unimportant things means that you can say yes to important things: the things you want to do, that need doing and that you like doing.

9
Declutter Information

There are so many different ways that information creeps into our lives: through print media, broadcast media and the internet. If you're like many of us, you read, listen to and watch the news. You read books and blogs, magazines and papers. You probably watch films, dramas and documentaries, reality TV and comedy. Maybe you listen to the radio and podcasts.

You have texts and emails, letters, notices and adverts. You may belong to one or more online forums, newsgroups or mailing lists. And, of course, there's Facebook, Twitter, Instagram and a number of other social media sites.

It's information overload!

Too much information has the same effect on your brain as physical clutter: it's overwhelming, stressful and frustrating. What do you do? Stop reading, listening and watching anything and everything? Of course not. But you *can* declutter your information consumption.

To start with, identify how many different types of media you use. Which of these do you read, listen to and watch in any one week?

- Texts
- Emails
- Newspapers
- Magazines
- Books
- Blogs
- Social media: Facebook, Twitter, Instagram
- Radio
- TV
- YouTube
- Films
- Documentaries.

Next, try making a note of how much time you spend reading and replying to texts and emails. How much time do you spend reading newspapers, magazines, books, blogs and social media sites? How much time do you spend watching TV, films and YouTube clips? Try logging the time you spend on media for one day.

Top Tip: Ask yourself what most draws you into your phone: apps? Texts? Emails? Facebook?

Set limits

See if you can cut out everything for a day; everything that isn't completely essential. If it's not work related, don't read it, watch it or listen to it. Just for a day or two. Pick a day you can do other activities – over the weekend maybe.

Disconnect; get used to being without your phone, tablet or laptop. Then try it for a couple of days. See if you can last. At least give it a try. You don't have to cut yourself off from the world. But if you *are* worried about missing out on what's going on in the world, ask somebody.

Don't let information take over your life. Set limits. Most of us have a number of sources of information that we could eliminate with no detriment to our lives whatsoever. Reduce the number of things that you read each day: cut down your consumption of news, television, Facebook, Twitter, Instagram etc. Delete every non-essential app. Instead of letting information take over your life, control how and when you receive it by limiting what you read, watch and listen to.

Set a limit for how many people you follow on social media – Facebook and Twitter – or how many apps you own. There will always be more information available than you can consume. Set limits so you're not simply trying to get through it all but, rather, enjoying more of what you consume.

Top Tip: When it comes to holidays, try a new approach to dealing with that post-holiday email mountain. A standard out-of-office message usually says: 'I'm now away until ... and will deal with your email on my return.' Instead, leave this message. 'Many thanks for your mail. Unfortunately I won't be able to read it, as I am away until ... and all my emails will be automatically deleted. Please email again after that date.'

Declutter your computer. Get rid of files and programs on your computer that you don't need. Clear most or all of the icons on your desktop. They not only slow down your computer, but they also create visual clutter. Regularly purge old, unused files.

Find other ways to spend your time

Whatever will you do with your time if you're not consuming information? What will you do if you're not spending so much time in front of a screen? The best way not to be in front of a media screen is simply to be somewhere else!

Get out more. Whether it's walking, going to the gym, rock climbing, taking part in a sport or relaxing yoga, get out more. Get some fresh air. Go hiking or cycling. Take a phone but turn it off.

Leave your desk at lunchtime. Unplug: switch off and go for a walk or, if there's a pool near you, go for a swim. Try leaving your phone at your desk.

Stretch your mind. Play board games or do individual puzzles. Organize games nights, play with others and be more sociable. Or do individual puzzles: crosswords, sudoku, etc.

Create things. We're all creative in some way. Instead of reading about or staring at things other people create, create your own things: art, words, music, recipes or a garden, for example. Learn to do something at your local adult education centre – painting, drawing, calligraphy, photography, pottery, etc.

Meet people. Get involved! Volunteer or join 'MeetUp' groups. Instead of getting close to a screen, get close to people.

Top Tip: Find a like-minded friend who is willing to join you in reducing information and media use. If you're part of a family, make it a family goal. It's important that each of you sets your own ideas of what makes for a reduction in media and information. Your ideas and aims may be different from another person's, but the important thing is that you support each other's efforts.

Positive news and information

Use your media intake more thoughtfully from now on. See if you can live with less: less social media, apps, radio, TV etc. None of these things are good or bad, it's what and how much you access the information they provide.

Instead of consuming whatever is readily available, clutters your mind and drains you, make more conscious choices about what you read, watch and listen to. Minimize the amount of negative news in your life. You're rarely better informed, your life isn't better off and you rarely feel better about yourself, other people or the world around you for having read low-level negative information.

Whether it's the economy, for example, or war and terrorism, the behaviour of celebrities or political scandal, you have little or no control over, but you can easily consume more and more information about them. This drains your time and energy and can leave you feeling stressed, helpless and negative simply *because* you have little or no control over these events.

Look for stories about people that inspire you. Don't read about people who are portrayed as victims, where the focus is on the unfairness of their situation and nothing seems to get resolved. Instead, read and listen to stories about people who are inspiring; who have made a contribution to others, who have demonstrated acts of kindness and compassion or who have coped admirably with adversity and bounced back.

Steer clear of negative headlines and dire tales of things going wrong. Look instead for uplifting stories that celebrate the best of life and be inspired by the good in the world around us.

Watch and read motivational stories or speeches. TED talks, for example (www.ted.com), are inspiring, educational and motivating. Online, you can find websites dedicated to sharing inspiring and positive news from around the world – www.dailygood.org is one. There are others listed in the 'Useful Websites' section of this book.

In a nutshell

- Too much information has the same effect on your brain as physical clutter: it's overwhelming, stressful and frustrating.
- Most of us have a number of sources of information that we could eliminate with no detriment to our lives whatsoever.
- You *can* declutter your information consumption. Identify how many different types of media you use. Then try making a note of how much time you spend consuming information; try logging your time spent on media for one day.
- See if you can cut out everything for a day, everything that isn't completely essential. If it's not work related, don't read it, watch it or listen to it. Just for a day or

two. Pick a day you can do other activities – over the weekend maybe. Then try it for a couple of days in the week. Give it a try.

- There will always be more information available than you can consume. Set limits so you're not simply trying to get through it all but, rather, enjoying more of what you consume.
- Find other ways to spend your time: get out more; meet people; do things that stretch your mind, not clutter it up; create things.
- Instead of consuming whatever is readily available, clutters your mind and drains you, make more conscious choices about what you read, watch and listen to.
- Steer clear of negative headlines and dire tales of things going wrong. Look instead for uplifting stories that celebrate the best of life and be inspired by the good in the world around us.

About the Author

Gill Hasson is a teacher, trainer and writer. She has 20 years' experience in the area of personal development. Her expertise is in the areas of confidence and self-esteem, communication skills, assertiveness and resilience.

Gill delivers teaching and training for educational organizations, voluntary and business organizations, and the public sector.

Gill is the author of the bestselling *Mindfulness* and *Emotional Intelligence* plus other books on the subjects of dealing with difficult people, resilience, communication skills and assertiveness.

Gill's particular interest and motivation is in helping people to realize their potential, to live their best life! You can contact Gill via her website www.gillhasson.co.uk or email her at gillhasson@btinternet.com.

Useful Websites

Experience Gifts
Redletterdays   Hundreds of ideas for 'experience' gifts.
www.redletterdays.co.uk

Social Groups
Meetup   Find and join groups of people in your local area who share your interests. There are groups to fit a wide range of interests and hobbies, plus others you'll never have thought of!
www.meetup.com

Positive, Inspiring News and Ideas
TED   Talks from expert speakers on education, business, science, tech and creativity
www.ted.com
www.dailygood.org/
www.huffingtonpost.com/topic/good-news/
www.goodnewsnetwork.org/
positivenews.org.uk/
www.sunnyskyz.com/

Hoarding

In May 2013, hoarding was officially recognized as a medical diagnosis. This means that help is available on the NHS. The following all have information and advice on managing a hoarding problem.

Mind
www.mind.org.uk

AgeUK
www.ageuk.org.uk

NHS
www.nhs.uk

Index

Index